Trans* Lives in the

Being and becoming trans* is a complex and varied experience whether an individual is living openly as trans* or not. Few published studies in either the academic or popular press illuminate the challenges of living as a trans* person after medical and social transition are complete. *Trans* Lives in the United States* builds upon earlier research and contributes a much-needed theoretically grounded empirical study that examines the hurdles from transition to the end of life by employing an intersectional analytical frame. The analysis pays careful attention to the role of class inequality, and draws on critical race studies, sexuality studies, and feminist studies. Drawing upon thirty face-to-face interviews, it privileges the experiences and voices of trans* individuals from a wide range of racial, ethnic, and class backgrounds. Moving beyond earlier studies that ended with an analysis of the moment of identity transition, this text provides a more nuanced understanding of the complex negotiations that individuals who self-identify as trans* endure.

Andrew Cutler-Seeber is an openly trans*-identified scholar. He earned his doctorate in Sociology with a doctoral emphasis in Feminist Studies at the University of California, Santa Barbara. Andrew teaches courses in Sociology, Social Work, and Trans* Studies. He lives in St. Croix, US Virgin Islands with his wife, Haley.

Framing 21st Century Social Issues
Series Editor: France Winndance Twine, University of California, Santa Barbara

The goal of this new, unique series is to offer readable, teachable "thinking frames" on today's social problems and social issues by leading scholars. These are available for view on http://routledge.customgateway.com/routledge-social-issues.html.

For instructors teaching a wide range of courses in the social sciences, the Routledge *Social Issues Collection* now offers the best of both worlds: originally written short texts that provide "overviews" to important social issues *as well as* teachable excerpts from larger works previously published by Routledge and other presses.

As an instructor, click to the website to view the library and decide how to build your custom anthology and which thinking frames to assign. Students can choose to receive the assigned materials in print and/or electronic formats at an affordable price.

Available

Trans* Lives in the United States
Challenges of Transition and Beyond
Andrew Rene Cutler-Seeber

Entrepreneurs and the Search for the American Dream
Zulema Valdez

The Global Beauty Industry
Colorism, Racism, and the National Body
Meeta Rani Jha

Trans* Lives in the United States
Challenges of Transition and Beyond

Andrew Cutler-Seeber

Routledge
Taylor & Francis Group

NEW YORK AND LONDON

First published 2018
by Routledge
711 Third Avenue, New York, NY 10017

and by Routledge
2 Park Square, Milton Park, Abingdon, Oxon, OX14 4RN

Routledge is an imprint of the Taylor & Francis Group, an informa business

Library of Congress Cataloging-in-Publication Data
A catalog record for this book has been requested

ISBN: 978-1-138-29668-8 (hbk)
ISBN: 978-1-138-29669-5 (pbk)
ISBN: 978-1-315-09983-5 (ebk)

Typeset in Adobe Garamond
by Florence Production Ltd, Stoodleigh, Devon, UK

Contents

Series Foreword

The first decades of the 21st century have been a time of paradoxes. We have witnessed a vibrant human rights movement that has advanced the civil rights of women, ethnic minorities, religious minorities and members of the LGBTQ, all during a period in which there is increasing economic inequality in some regions, climate change, and mass migration because of civil wars, religious conflicts, and state violence. The 21st century has also witnessed a resurgence of earlier forms of racism, nativism, white nationalism and violence (in Asia, Africa, the Americas, Europe, and the Middle East), against vulnerable populations including girls, women and individuals perceived to be sexual dissidents. Sociologists offer theories, concepts and analytical frames that enable us to better understand the challenges and cultural transformations of the twenty-first century. In doing so, they generate new forms of collective knowledge that can help solve some of our local, global and transnational problems.

This is the seventh year of our Routledge "Framing 21 Century Social Issues" series. Our series includes books on a wide range of topics including climate change, consumption, torture, entrepreneurship, assisted reproductive technologies, and the global beauty industry. These books all explore contemporary social problems in ways that introduce basic sociological concepts, cover key literature in the field, and offer original interpretations and diagnoses. They also intervene in current debates within the social sciences over how to best define, rethink and respond to the social concerns that preoccupy the early 21st century.

The goal of this series is to provide accessible essays that examine a wide range of social issues with local, global, and transnational impact. Sociologists are ideally poised to cotribute to a global conversation on issues spanning state violence, migration, militarism, class inequality, the impact of mass incarceration on local economies, medical technologies, health disparities and environmental degradation. The contributors to this series bring the works of classical sociology into dialogue with contemporary social theorists from diverse theoretical traditions including, but not limited to, critical race theory, feminist, Marxist and European social theory.

Readers do not need an extensive background in academic sociology to benefit from these books. Each one is student-friendly in that we provide glossaries of terms for the uninitiated that are connected to bolded terms in the text. Each chapter ends with questions for further thought and discussion. The books are ideal for undergraduates because they are accessible without sacrificing a theoretically sophisticated and innovative analysis.

Andrew Cutler-Seeber provides the first sociological analysis of the lives of trans individuals that is intersectional. This book considers the life cycle of trans individuals from diverse racial, ethnic, class, and regional backgrounds. It provides a much-needed corrective to the monochromatic representations of middle and upper middle class white trans individuals who are celebrities and thus, not representative of the experiences of a diverse group of people. The challenges, complexities, and class-based struggles of trans individuals, after transition, have received little attention in either the academic or popular press. Moreover, the ways that racial and class inequality structure the experiences of trans individuals have been neglected and missing from earlier discussions. This book provides a much- needed intersectional analysis of the struggles of trans individuals, who live in all regions of the mainland United States. It will inspire complex discussions of how trans people negotiate their social, sexual, medical and economic needs during different life stages. It is ideal for courses in the sociology of sex, gender, sociology of the body and social psychology.

France Winddance Twine
Series Editor

Preface

Trans* for Life

An estimated 1.4 million **trans*** people currently reside in the United States, which amounts to roughly 0.6% of the country's population. The percentage of young people, age 18–24, is higher at 0.7% than for people in the 25–64 age bracket, 0.6%, or the 65 and older bracket in which 0.5% identify as trans* (Flores et al. 2016). According to a 2016 survey of public opinion on **transgender** rights in 23 countries, the United States ranked ninth in support for transgender rights. The ranking was based on support for six areas: transition surgery, changing identification documents, discrimination protection, access to restrooms of current identity, the right to marry, adopt, and give birth. Nearly 72% of American survey participants (n=1,000) agreed that transgender people should have government protection from discrimination and roughly 73% agreed that trans* individuals should be allowed to surgically transition their bodies (Flores, Brown, and Park 2016).

A growing body of interdisciplinary literature has been produced since the 1990s that examines early medical transition and identity transformation of trans* individuals—people who identify as **transsexual**, transgender, or sex and/or **gender non-conforming**. However, being and becoming trans* does not end after the completion of any physical modifications. Neither the academic nor popular press has provided much insight into the *life-long consequences and challenges* of being a trans* individual, even if a person no longer identifies as trans*. In this book, I offer a theoretically grounded empirical case study that builds upon earlier research in the United States. I provide an analysis of the period of transition itself and the ongoing challenges and dilemmas that trans* individuals endure over the course of their lives. Furthermore, I apply an intersectional analytical lens, which distinguishes this book from the memoirs, and earlier books that focused primarily upon middle and upper middle class White Americans.

This book is organized and motivated by the following questions: 1) How does a trans* identity continue to affect an individual after the initial intensity of physical and social transition itself has subsided? 2) Why do these complications continue to take place? 3) How do individuals manage the difficulties that may arise? 4) How do intersecting identities of race, class, sex, and gender impact the frequency and kinds of challenges individuals face? 5). What resources can individuals utilize to negotiate these circumstances? This project assumes that giving voice to trans* self-understandings and perspectives beyond transition is crucial to broadening awareness of and support for trans* people throughout their lives and in a way that is attentive to differences between individuals created by simultaneously held identities.

It is also worth noting that my own trans* identity is relevant to this text. Having transitioned away from the female identity I was assigned at birth, I have an insider status within trans* communities. This has provided me with first-hand knowledge about the trans* experience which proved helpful in gaining access to and rapport with research participants. I recognize that people hold a wide variety of trans* identities and that each individual experiences being trans* in different ways. At the same time, my identity initiated a sense of community with and investment in understanding and telling these stories as authentically and compassionately as possible.

The first chapter introduces a concept that I term the **paradox of (trans*)identity**—that is, the awareness of trans* people that while their sex and/or gender identity may not fall into one of the two commonly accepted categories or has changed categories over time, they live in a society that assumes sex and gender are both binary and unchangeable. I detail the theoretical contribution to sex and gender theory and distinguish between sex and gender both as concepts and identities. I include the use of one text from trans* studies literature as an example of why this distinction is necessary. This chapter lays the foundation necessary for the following chapter on embodied capital.

Chapter Two builds upon the recent work of feminist race scholars (Brooks, Twine, Hunter), who have expanded Pierre Bourdieu's concept of capital to include embodied capital. I introduce the concept of **gender congruence capital**, which is the *power that flows from possessing a sex identity that* **"matches"** *one's gender identity*. I then discuss **sex category capital**, *the power of being identified easily as a male or female, rather than ambiguous by others*.

Chapter Three draws upon the lives of fourteen individuals to argue that internal hierarchies in trans* communities can operate to further stigmatize some trans* individuals. I identify two narratives that I term *"trans*-er than thou"* perspectives. I then examine the relationships between intersecting identities of sex, gender, race, and class and these two trans* narratives. I highlight the way in which trans* communities also include and reflect the hierarchies of race that exist in the broader U.S. society. The chapter concludes by describing how all of these hierarchies contribute to the continued mainstream exclusion of trans* people.

Chapter Four is the first of three chapters focused on specific areas of life where the *paradox of (trans*)identity* generates challenges in the lives of trans* people. This chapter draws on the experiences of three **trans* females** and one **trans* male** to illuminate the relationships trans* people have with the families that raised them as well as the families they created before transitioning. Drawing on an additional five cases, I provide an analysis of the ways in which trans* identity informs the experiences of dating and forming intimate relationships after transition. The chapter concludes by exploring the nuanced relationship between sex identity, gender identity, and sexual orientation.

Chapter Five addresses challenges in the areas of employment and housing. This chapter draws upon the experiences of ten trans* people who live in diverse regions of the United States to examine how occupational challenges structure the work lives of trans* people. I examine the historical occupational options as well as the unpredictability of employment and the unique challenges associated with working as a trans*-identified person. Parallels between housing and employment are explored in terms of *"status" checks*, that is the checking of references in employment and housing rental markets, and how these realities are affected by one's race and class status.

In Chapter Six I analyze the accessibility of healthcare for trans* people. Drawing upon the experiences of seven trans* individuals, I pay careful attention to the intersecting issues of race and class inequality that determine access to health resources. I discuss exclusions from health insurance coverage for treatment that insurance providers deem *"trans*-related,"* even when the treatment is not actually related to the person's trans* status. Drawing on the concerns of two trans* male participants I consider the future health needs of an aging trans* population. Finally, I examine issues regarding end-of-life decisions and respecting the dignity of trans* people in death.

In the Epilogue, I return to a discussion of the theoretical value of employing an intersectional analytical frame. As an example, I explore the race, class, sex, and gender realities of violence against trans* people. Furthermore, I point out the significance of analyzing life beyond transition in examining the lives and experiences of trans* people. I then briefly address the shifting realities of trans* people in many areas of life including military service, changes to health insurance under the Affordable Care Act, the backlash of "bathroom bills" targeting the rights and safety of trans* people, and the implications of Title VII and Title IX legal interpretations of "sex discrimination."

Acknowledgments

I would like to thank the many people who opened their homes and life stories to me, making this project possible. Your time, good humor, and generosity are much appreciated. This text began as a dissertation project for which I would like to thank my committee, Verta Taylor, France Winddance Twine, Alicia Cast, and Leila Rupp for their hours of work, attention, and support in guiding me through the research and writing process. I have many colleagues and friends to thank, especially Noa Klein and Elizabeth Rahilly, for places to sleep, challenging conversations, and continuous cheerleading throughout the process of researching, interviewing, organizing, and writing the original project.

Turning a dissertation into a book takes many hours of added work and support. I especially thank France Winddance Twine for endless hours of advice, editing, mentorship, and guidance in this endeavor—I could not ask for a better friend and colleague. I also thank Dean Birkenkamp for believing in this project from the start and championing it to publication. For the reading and editing of multiple drafts of chapters, invaluable insights, and intellectual debates over linguistic differences, I have my dear friend Lindley Graham to thank. I also greatly appreciate and thank Jesse Klein for her friendship and fine-tuned copy editing skills. I would like to thank my family for always being there and supporting me from afar, even when I confused them with pronouns, needed a place to visit for breaks, or asked them to travel completely across the country for my wedding. Finally, I would like to thank my wonderful wife, Haley Cutler-Seeber, for her inspiration, support, patience for graduate student life, and most importantly, her love.

1 Bodies and Behaviors

So I did the hormone thing. I was living as a woman, but feeling like I still wasn't . . . I still needed to feminize more. Some of the girls in the community, they had gone for the pumping, which is the black market injections. Very prevalent in the trans*[1] community. Very prevalent. For years it's been that way. It was almost like a rite of passage. I hate to even call it that. A lot of us girls do not have the money to do it the right way. The right way would be to go to a certified plastic surgeon and have all that facial feminization surgery done, which costs thousands. Breast implants, thousands. You know, it's just so much cost. Economically, that social economical status that a lot of us trans* girls fall into, it's real and it's a reality. You're trying to make something happen that's so important to you because it's almost like life or death— matching the way you look on the outside with the way you feel on the inside—with two pennies.

—Nima

Nima[2] was a 48-year-old trans* female activist. The daughter of a multiracial (French, Black, and Native American) mother and an Indian father from Trinidad, she identified as "mixed-race." While her mother might be categorized by others as White, Nima had a rich caramel complexion, having inherited darker skin from her "100% East Indian" biological father. She had brown curly hair and brown eyes, a round face, curvaceous figure, and was dressed in a sleeve-less, colorful print dress during the interview. Nima had an infectiously positive outlook and strong, powerful spirit that spoke with great wisdom, clarity, and compassion. She lived on less than $15,000 a year, based on pay from her various speaking engagements as an activist. Nima's story shows how **race**, **class**, and body procedures are co-produced.

Years ago, poor and feeling the pressure for facial feminization treatments in order to leave a more **androgynous** space and its challenges, Nima turned to a trans* community insider providing treatments referred to as "**pumping**"—the injection of silicone into the skin. Knowing that professional services and cosmetic surgery were safer, but far out of economic reach, she found someone recommended by others as having done this type of work with good results for several years.

Believing that she was receiving injections of medical-grade silicon from a knowledgeable, but unlicensed practitioner, Nima began treatment. Her goal was to round and soften her facial features. Using the same methods, she began to enlarge her breasts, thighs, and buttocks to create a more curvaceous figure in line with stereotypical ideals of conventional female bodies. After 7 months of treatment, nodules as hard as rocks formed in her face surrounded by a life-threatening infection around the injection sites and Nima found out the silicone was actually a mixture of industrial-grade silicone. By then, the damage was done.

Several years of kind and graciously cheap treatment by certified plastic surgeons to soften the silicone in her skin improved her appearance considerably. Still, the "pumping" caused significant disfiguration and the surgeons felt that any attempts to remove the mixture would be far too dangerous and potentially fatal. "Pumping" made impossible the gain in status Nima had hoped to achieve, even though she left behind being viewed by others as somewhere in between male and female. Growing up as an outsider because of her mixed-race background and "unmanly ways," Nima found herself marginalized and poor. Unlike her upper middle class trans* peers who could afford to pay for licensed care, Nima reached out to the best she could find affordably. Because transition-related surgery is rarely covered by health insurance, income makes a significant difference in the type of care available to trans* people. The disfigurement caused by pumping contributed to Nima's ongoing economic instability.

Don Kulick discussed the practice of pumping in *Travestí: Sex, Gender and Culture among Brazilian Trans-gendered Prostitutes* (1998), where it was clear that those partaking were aware the injections were of industrial-grade silicone. Travestí, a Brazilian Portuguese word, refers to people assigned male at birth who are interested in relationships with males in which they are the penetrated partner, who also modify their bodies to be more female and "do gender" in a feminine fashion. Travestí are not synonymous with transsexuals in the United States.[3] Travestí often purchased the silicone themselves, and created apparatuses like halters or used plastic wrap (for heat) and pantyhose (for compression) to get the silicone to work into the body in the ways they wished. Speaking with Nima, it turned out that the practice of pumping was also quite common within the United States, particularly among those who could not afford the higher cost of professional cosmetic surgeries and treatments. But as Nima pointed out, here in the United States she was made to believe the silicone being used was medical-grade.

Initially suffering from frequent bouts of clinical depression as a result of the disfigurement, Nima found a purpose and silver lining in her troubles. Nima shared her experiences with others as a cautionary tale. She urged others worldwide who found themselves in similar financial straits and in dire need of identity-affirming physical changes to hold on to hope for better, less risky solutions, or at least tried to help them understand how serious the risks are that need to be weighed. As she put it, "Getting the black market injections, or pumping as we call it, can be a girl's best friend or a girl's worst enemy. Sometimes, for some girls, it can be a little bit of both." A kind, empathetic, larger-than-life spirit and personality, Nima became a fierce advocate for trans* people and an inspiration to people the world over. If only the pay for an inspirational, multiracial, trans* female of color were higher.

Nima's story highlights issues that often go unaddressed in the popular media portrayals of celebrity trans* people. While audiences are fascinated with the anxiety, fear, discrimination, and courage of trans* people expressed in the media spotlight, the economic costs and symbolic and social capital required to live a healthy trans* life are seldom explored. These types of capital provide forms of privilege that are central to the transitions and stories of trans* individuals highlighted in the media—privileges Nima did not possess and which are only available to a select few of the roughly 1.4 million trans*-identified people living in the United States (Flores et al. 2016).

In addition to the ability to finance hormone therapy, surgeries, medical care, and time off work, celebrities like Caitlyn Jenner, Chaz Bono, and Lana Wachowski[4] also benefited from White privilege with regard to the social acceptance they received during their sex and gender transitions. As White elites, Jenner, Bono, and Wachowski were able to strategically navigate the media and popular press to boost their social capital, gaining significant advantages when compared to their impoverished and working-class peers such as Nima. As Joshua Gamson (1998) pointed out in *Freaks Talk Back: Tabloid Talk Shows and Sexual Non-Conformity*, previous generations of trans* people may have made inroads in the media through shows like Jerry Springer and Sally Jessy Raphael during the 1980s and 1990s. However these shows were designed to be salacious, sensationalistic, and painted less than positive pictures of trans* people.

It is important to celebrate and support trans* celebrities like Jenner, Bono, and Wachowski in their moves to live life as their most authentic selves. However, believing these stories to be representative of a much larger trans* population would hardly do justice to the thousands of equally valid identities and experiences of a very diverse population known collectively as trans*.

Trans* Identity, Literature, and Missing Pieces

The interdisciplinary scholarship on trans* identity emerged as a field and became consolidated at the beginning of the 1990s.[5] For example, in 1994, Kate Bornstein published *Gender Outlaw: On Men, Women, and the Rest of Us*, beginning a conversation about trans* identity from the perspective of trans* identified people. Since the 1990s, a great deal of scholarship across a variety of disciplines has been produced by and about trans* people. From this scholarship we gained an understanding of how trans* people came to be, in terms of their identity development (Devor 2004; Diamond, Pardo, and Butterworth 2011), and how they understood themselves in society (Devor 1997, 2004; Diamond, Pardo, and Butterworth 2011; Meyerowitz 2002; Prosser 1998; Rubin 2003; Serano 2007). We also gained a sense of their theoretical importance, use, and misuse as models for understanding gender and how it operates in daily life (Butler [1990] 2007, [1993] 2011; Dozier 2005; Fausto-Sterling 2000; Namaste 2000; Yavorsky 2016). Additionally we have literature that examined the justification and defense of the trans* person's right to exist and define the self (Stryker and Aizura 2013; Stryker and Whittle 2006).

Despite the wealth of scholarship that now exists on the trans* experience, there remain a number of limitations in this literature. First, trans* people are relatively invisible as *trans** people after transition, in both sociological literature as well as the interdisciplinary field of trans* studies. Second, there is a dearth of intersectional analysis in trans* literature.[6] Few studies detail the ways that age, race, class, sex, gender, and appearance norms structure the experience of transition itself as well as life after transition.[7]

I respond to these limitations by first explaining why it is that trans* identity continues to matter, whether or not someone is visibly or openly trans*. Second, I provide a sustained and nuanced intersectional analysis of the ways that age, appearance, sex, gender, race, and class privilege structure the trans* experience. Finally, I address difficulties that persist in attending to distinctions between **sex**, **sex category**, and **gender** as well as in the ability of current literature to address complexities of **nonbinary** sex and gender.

Because sex and gender are assumed to be binary and fixed in our society, information that challenges these ideas, that a person is trans* for example, can disturb people's assumptions about sex and gender (Burke and Stets 2009). As a result, trans* people have a more difficult time with **identity verification**. This means that when compared to **cisgender/cissexual**[8] (**cis***) people, trans* individuals face more challenges having their identities correctly acknowledged by others.[9]

Trans* people then are experiencing what I call a paradox of (trans*)identity in that they are living proof that sex and/or gender are neither binary nor fixed though they live within a society that operates as if sex and/or gender *are* binary and fixed. This paradox and the disruption it causes in identity verification occurs whether or not the trans* person identifies as binary, meaning male *and* masculine or female *and* feminine. Binary or not, the trans* person knows they operate in a world that makes a binary assumption. If a trans* person currently identifies as and appears binary, any situations that make a previous sex and/or gender identity known disrupts how others perceive the trans* person's identity. This happens because people are provided information incongruent with the trans* person's current identity.

For some trans* people, their identity contains non-binary understandings of their own sex and gender, for example people who identify as both male and female, a third sex option, **intersex** by design, gender non-conforming, etc. For others, they have a sense of their sex and/or gender identity changing over time, such as a specifically trans* identity, sometimes masculine and/or sometimes feminine cross-dresser, or previously male now female, etc. In both of these situations as well, verification of the trans* person's current identity also fails to occur. In these instances, it is because others are working from the assumption that sex and gender categories are binary and fixed, even though this is not the trans* person's experience.

The non-binary identified person is more likely to face disruptions in getting their identity verified by others on a regular basis if their non-binary identities are visible. If a trans* person is binary identified *and* visibly binary, they might more frequently be able to avoid this disturbance (and the salience of their trans* identity), except in instances where their history of sex and gender identities are revealed or become relevant to the situation.

What Can We Learn From Critical Race Studies and Specifically Whiteness Studies?

How can we understand how the White celebrity's transition and later-life experiences of trans* identity differ from those of individuals who belong to racial or ethnic minorities and/or are not qualified for inclusion in the White category? From the many trans* people I spoke with for this project, there was a necessary imperative to think through the role that race and class played in how a trans* identity was asserted, experienced, and achieved. Critiques posed about the racial and **socioeconomic** privileges many celebrity trans* people have were based in an ongoing historical, intellectual examination of the production of Whiteness, White identity, and the role of White identity in the reproduction of racial and class inequality. Whiteness studies was a product of Black Studies, whose intellectual antecedents were found in the late nineteenth and early twentieth century theoretical work of W.E.B. DuBois (Twine and Gallagher 2008; Twine and Steinbugler 2006). Beginning with the observation that marginalized Whites in the reconstruction era cast their lot with dominant Whites rather than with similarly class-marginalized Blacks, DuBois started an exploration of the "wages" of Whiteness. He also pointed out how a lack of individually felt prejudice helped maintain the functioning of Whiteness as invisible to Whites (Twine and Gallagher 2008).

During the **second wave of feminism**, which began in the early 1960s, and the **Civil Rights Era**,[10] Black feminists challenged racial, sexual, and gender discrimination in both movements. Within the Civil Rights Movement, Black males often dismissed the concerns of Black feminists and perceived issues with sexism as secondary to issues of racism (Barnett 1993; Crawford, Rouse, and Woods 1990; Robnett 1997). Within the mainstream Women's Movement, some White feminists conceptualized their issues as women as universal and as separate from issues of racism (Crenshaw 1989; Frankenberg 1993; hooks 1984; Hull, Bell-Scott, and Smith 1982).

In 1978, the **Combahee River Collective** published its iconic treatise on intersectional analysis declaring:

> The most general statement of our politics at the present time would be that we are actively committed to struggling against racial, sexual, heterosexual, and class oppression and see as our particular task the development of integrated analysis and practice based upon the fact that the major systems of oppression are interlocking.
>
> (362)

Noting that their "experience and disillusionment within these liberation movements ... led to the need to develop a politics that was antiracist, unlike those of White women, and antisexist, unlike those of Black and White men," the Collective and other like-minded racial and ethnic minority feminists began an intersectional approach to oppression (Combahee River Collective 1978: 363; Crenshaw 1991; Hull, Bell-Scott, and Smith 1982). The importance of understanding that people hold multiple identities simultaneously is clearly relevant to the study of trans* people, considering that trans* is only one of many identities claimed by people in this study.

Patricia Hill Collins' (2004) discussion of gender ideologies specified by race and class is useful here in understanding the dissimilar experiences of differently situated trans* people. Collins argued that middle-class Black men are viewed as emasculated side-kicks and comic relief, while working-class Black men are seen as dangerous, threatening, criminal menaces to society. Black women, Collins asserted, are classified as the working-class jezebel/bad mother threat to sexual propriety and family, or the middle-class "Modern Mammies, Black Ladies, and 'Educated Bitches'" who are ambitious, but non-threatening to White or patriarchal society (2004: 138).

Kevin was a 33-year-old Black trans* male with a mustache, beard, and almost clean-shaven head. The son of a Juris Doctorate (JD) father and a mother with a PhD in child psychology, he grew up in a middle-class family in rural and suburban areas of Northern Florida, in the cultural South. Kevin's experiences called attention to one dimension of transitioning that disproportionately affected Black trans* males. He adjusted from being, in his perspective, relatively invisible to mainstream White society. Later, as a hyper-visible and hyper-sexualized Black male, Kevin had to negotiate a range of denigrating and derogatory stereotypes organized around the myth of the dangerous Black man:

It's strange going from being a relatively invisible Black lesbian to being a hyper-visible Black man. I think it was—this was a few years ago—I was walking down [a busy] street with a backpack and a hoodie on and this lady damn near broke her neck trying to get off the sidewalk with me. She was a White woman. She was clutching her purse. She was definitely afraid and that was a turning point in my life where I realized that okay, things are different now.

Next, consider the trajectory of Ryzha, a 36-year-old Black and Native American trans* female, who spent her young life as the living image of emasculated side-kick White society has imagined for Black males. Growing up, Ryzha was bullied and beaten by both Blacks and Whites as an affront to masculinity, and a particular affront to Black masculinity built in opposition to White stereotypes. Later, living as her authentic self, Ryzha was treated as either visibly trans*—epitomizing the betrayal of Black masculinity in a White supremacist society and the "**walking while trans***"[11] threat to sexual propriety—or the invisible Black lady. Seated in the hot humid entry room of a friend's apartment, wearing cutoff jean shorts, a coral tank top, and a long brown straight-haired wig when I met her, Ryzha shared with me:

I always tell people when I talk to them it's like I have three strikes against me. From furthest away you see that I'm a Black person and in our society, that's something that is one strike. Then . . . you see that I'm a woman which is another one. Then . . . you may see I'm trans*, so there's those three strikes . . . I mean you have a certain stereotype when it comes to a trans* woman of color . . . When a person first meets me they're expecting the ghetto, ratchet type of personality, uneducated, all about nails and hair and all of that stuff and not seeing any other option that a trans* woman of color can be. Educated and learned, and well-spoken, talented and any of those other things. It's a barrier that I usually have to break through when I'm entering any new social situation.

In the United States, **structural racism** and classism shape the entire life cycle—determining who has privileged access to resources and experiences (on health see Smedley 2012, Thomas et al. 2011; on mortality see Miniño et al. 2009; on education see Snyder, de Brey, and Dillow 2016, U.S. Bureau of the Census 2015). For example, Gilbert Gee, Katrina Walsemann, and Elizabeth Brondolo pointed out:

> . . . racism in the form of residential and school segregation may influence the development of social networks, which may then shape employment opportunities and health. One study suggested that youths attending racially isolated high schools were more likely to work in racially isolated workplaces in adulthood, even after accounting for residential segregation, region, school, and personal resources.
>
> (2012: 967–968)

The multiple status positions (race/class/sex/gender/sexuality/age) that trans* individuals hold requires an intersectional analysis, particularly when trying to understand the experiences of transition and post-transition life.

Distinguishing Between Sex and Gender Identities

Gender Theory

Theorization in gender studies within humanities and the social sciences has generally adhered to one of two main strains of thought: **poststructuralist/queer theory's** performativity, or the **sociological interactional/accountability** "doing gender" approach (Namaste 2000). I will briefly outline the advancements gained from each approach, then explain my own contribution to gender theory and why it is necessary to understanding the **embodied capital** experienced by trans* people.

The poststructuralist/queer theory approach focused on the **performativity** of gender, a theory explicated by Judith Butler beginning in the 1980s (Butler 1988). From this perspective we learned that gender was something that all human beings perform within the prescribed parameters of their cultural and historical location. The importance of gender and our performance of it reduced the importance of the body in interaction, as biological characteristics were made equivalent to non-biological aspects of performance. This approach also suggested that our understandings of sex are actually shaped by notions of gender. For example, Anne Fausto-Sterling (2000) proposed, "Our conceptions of the nature of gender difference shape, even as they reflect, the ways we structure our social system and polity; they also shape and reflect our understanding of physical bodies" (45). In this vein, the idea that bodies are less relevant than beliefs about gender behavior was further underscored by the great deal of overlap that exists in bodily characteristics across the sexes (see for example Fausto-Sterling 2000). Some females are taller than some males and some males have less body hair than some females, even though on average males are taller and have more body hair. The idea that there is so much overlap in bodily characteristics, combined with Butler's (1988) assertion that, "considering that 'the' body is invariably transformed into his body or her body, the body is only known through its gendered appearance" (523), suggested that the ways we *perform* gender are more important than our female and/or male bodily characteristics in regards to how we function as sexed and gendered beings in daily life.

The sociological interactional/accountability approach known as "**Doing Gender**" was introduced by Candace West and Don Zimmerman (1987) at about the same time as the poststructuralist/queer theory approach. Further developed by many others in the proceeding years (e.g. Dozier 2005; Lorber 1994), this approach also focused on gender as something that everyone "does" at all times. It also specifically added that it is something we are all held accountable for doing on the basis of the sex category we are assumed to be. For example, if someone is perceived to be an incumbent in the female sex category, she is expected to not only dress, but also walk, talk, and do any number of things in a specifically feminine fashion. This perspective has provided scholars a great deal of insight into the process of gender socialization during childhood and how gender "gets done" in any situation, any environment or institution, throughout our entire lives. Notably, the original conceptualization of the "doing gender" framework was based on observations with someone identified by researchers as trans*, and then applied to an understanding of how gender operates for everyone (West and Zimmerman 1987).

While we have gained much from this approach, this research has largely focused on people who may be perceived as sex and gender congruent—meaning attributed by others as female *and* feminine—and/or were working toward congruency. Furthermore, in some recent research on trans* people and gender, those who may not be socially congruent—and may or may not wish to be—were categorized in ways that make them appear more congruent by labeling them as men and women. This can be seen for example in Schilt's (2010) work on trans* men where some informants viewed themselves as men while others did not identify in a binary fashion. In the latter cases, the informants may accurately be referred to as "not women," but "men" may be an inaccurate oversimplification (see McCall 2003 on this distinction between what "I am" and what "I am not"). By focusing on people who were or were striving to be sex and gender congruent, or by re-categorizing people into categories that made them seem more congruent, interactional/accountability theorists fell into a similar trap as those using the poststructuralist/queer theory perspective. In both perspectives, gender was privileged and the importance of bodily sex characteristics, or the visible secondary sex characteristics used to assign sex category in daily life, were eclipsed.

Gender theorists have examined the social activity of gender, while addressing sex category only insofar as it provides a point of reference for whether one is performing or doing gender properly—to judge femininity as correct by first assessing that an individual is female. However, it is especially important to attend to both bodies (sex) and behavior (gender) when examining the experiences of trans* people. Several trans*-identified scholars have pointed out the limitations of poststructuralist/queer theory and sociological interactional/accountability perspectives (see Devor 2004; Namaste 2000; Serano 2007). Viviane Namaste (2000) in particular has notably pointed out the shortcomings of both approaches. She noted that queer theory's approach to poststructuralism erased the reality of trans* lives by using subjects as representations of something else and not accounting for the context and realities of subjects' lives. As examples, Namaste examined works of Butler (1990 and 1993) and critiqued:

> Butler uses the example of drag queens in order to claim that all gender is socially constructed. Yet as we observed earlier, Butler's project is insufficient because she does not examine the institutional site in which the gendered performances of drag queens occur. In this manner, her citation of drag comes to stand in for sex/gender relations more broadly. Similarly, in her presentation of Venus Extravaganza from the film *Paris is Burning*, Butler's nebulous reference to the economic and social realities of Latina women in New York City enables her

to claim that Extravaganza is treated by the symbolic order in a manner similar to that of (nontranssexual) women of color.

(2000: 21)

Extravaganza, Namaste explained, "was killed because she was a transsexual prostitute," not because she was being treated as cis* women of color are treated in the structure of status and power in the United States (2000: 13). Namaste scathingly argued that "queer theory's epistemological and methodological presuppositions authorize a political agenda that robs transgendered people of dignity and integrity" (2000: 23).

If Namaste took queer theory and the use of poststructuralism by its practitioners to task, her explanation of the problems with the sociological interactional/accountability and social sciences approaches more broadly were nearly as disparaging. Pointing to a focus on the psychological and medical production of trans* people within sociological study, Namaste criticized sociological research as "primarily for academics, not for members of the research population, nor even for legislators, jurists, social policy experts, or the administrative personnel of community-based organizations that work with the individuals under investigation" (2000: 37). She went on to argue that several studies:

... clearly illustrate the arrogance that underlines so much academic sociology. Most of this scholarship assumes that transsexuals would not change their sex once they have read enough Marxist or feminist theory: a hypothesis that cannot account for the realities of individuals who change sex *after* exposure to Marxist, socialist, or feminist theories and politics ... Indeed, much social science establishes an opposition between liberated academics who understand the constructed nature of gender and the poor duped transsexuals who are victims of false consciousness.

(2000: 37–38)

In addition to her criticisms of the methods, assumptions, and utility of both poststructuralist/queer theory and sociological interactional/accountability approaches, Namaste (2000) explained that the body itself was important to identity as more than just an effect of "a sedimentation of gender norms" (Butler 1988: 524).

The Body

Scholars researching the body have also pointed to the increasing importance of the body as a personal project (Brumberg 1997; Pitts 2003; Shilling 2003). For example, Chris Shilling noted that the body was becoming a, "*project* which should be worked at and accomplished as part of an *individual's* self-identity" (2003: 4, emphasis in original). However, research on the body also tended to examine people who were congruent—male *and* masculine or female *and* feminine—or simply conflated sex and gender such that femininity was taken for granted as an element of being female.

Gender theory taught us that there was nothing about being male that necessitated masculinity nor female, femininity, and research on the body showed us the importance of the body to identity. Yet neither gender nor body theory separated **sex identity** and **gender identity** as simultaneous but separate, important identities. For example, what if someone was assigned male at birth and desired to be female, but had no interest in performing femininity? Author Jennifer Finney Boylan discussed this separation at length in her 2003 memoir *She's Not There: A Life in Two Genders*, although the title still made the sex/gender conflation. Boylan described her irritation with the expectation of femininity whereby females introduce themselves using an upward inflection, making a statement of their name sound like a question. However, while Boylan explained her sense of identifying as female and needing to make this identity her physical reality, she noted that this feminine inflection and many other expectations of femininity remained outside of her sense of authentic female self.

What if an individual wished to move from an assignment as female to something more male, but wanted to retain the same **genderqueer**[12] performance before and after bodily changes? How do we understand the separation of **body (sex) identity** and **behavior (gender) identity** if sex characteristics change, but not with sex and gender congruence as the end goal or outcome?

A Multilayer Binary

Whether privileging gender while eclipsing the body, or focusing on the body and taking gender for granted, attending to people who are sex and gender congruent lends itself to the conflation of sex and gender identities. I suggest that this conflation is reinforced by the use of the categories woman and man, which are neither categories of sex nor categories of gender. Instead, woman and man are categories that link female bodies to culturally prescribed behaviors that are defined as "feminine" and male bodies to "masculine" behaviors. The terms woman and man oversimplify a multilayer, "matched," or "congruent," binary. This multilayer binary is represented in Figure 1.1.

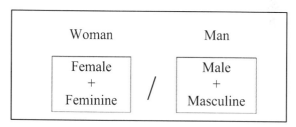

Woman		Man
Female + Feminine	/	Male + Masculine

Figure 1.1 The sex/gender binary

When scholars discuss the sex/gender binary, they typically use the category woman to refer to the first box and man to refer to the second. However, they are not simply referring to the sex binary of female/male. They are also not only referring to the gender binary femininity/masculinity. Instead they are referring to the compound sex/gender binary of female *and* feminine or male *and* masculine. The terms woman and man operate to tie sex and gender together, as in the earlier diagram, by pointing out that these categories can be qualified with regard to either sex or gender. For example, one may be a masculine woman, qualifying the gender component of the woman category while maintaining a tie to the category of woman through sex categorization as female. One may also be a transsexual woman, qualifying the sex component of the category. That we can qualify woman either in terms of gender or sex points out that woman as a category is neither one of sex nor gender entirely.

Trans* Studies

As examples of foundational texts in the field of trans* studies, Susan Stryker (2008) and Susan Stryker and Stephen Whittle (2006), showed that trans* studies has done a great deal to promote understanding of the separation between sexuality and gender, as well as sex and gender. From the mid-nineteenth century through the beginning of the twentieth century, sex, gender, and sexuality were understood as components of a single concept governed by biological determinism, where female led to femininity and an attraction to men (F→F→W4M),[13] or male led to masculinity and attraction to women (M→M→M4W). In this approach, "inversion" was used to describe deviation in any part of this linkage, whether that meant masculine females or people with same-sex desire (Stryker 2008). Within trans* studies these different ways of breaking down the sex/gender/sexuality linkage were viewed as separate issues, but like in many other fields, theorists still conflated the concepts of sex and gender through their use of "gender identity." Gender identity was defined from this perspective as one's internal sense of being a man or woman, regardless of what sex was assigned to the bodies they inhabited. But as I noted above, man and woman are problematic categories. In using woman or man as the internal sense referred to by "gender identity," are we talking about one's internal sense of their body (sex—male/female/intersex/other), or of their desired set of behaviors (gender—masculine/feminine/genderqueer/other)?

Trans* studies, then, has made strides in clarifying some conceptual distinctions, such as between sexuality and gender, and provided examples of people with a wide variety of identifications and perspectives (Stryker and Whittle 2006). However, as a field, it still largely combines a person's sense of their sexed body with their sense of behavioral fit under the single umbrella of "gender identity," as do many other fields in the humanities, social, and medical sciences. Although useful when considering people who are both cissexual and cisgender, when it comes to dealing with a variety of configurations of trans* people, the adherence to woman and man as categories becomes increasingly challenging. In particular, using woman and man is difficult when looking at the breakdown of identity verification discussed in sociological identity theory, and in understanding the relationship between sex, gender, and embodied capital as discussed in Chapter Two (Seeber 2013).

Trans* studies, along with social science and medical theories, tend to oversimplify the complexity of conceptually distinct, though simultaneously experienced, considerations: sex—a sense of bodily authenticity (as male, merm, herm, ferm, female, etc.; see Fausto-Sterling 2000); sex category—how what is visible of sex will be categorized in interaction; and gender—behavioral inclinations (masculinity, femininity, gender variant, genderqueer, etc.). As with cis* people, each of these three considerations will not necessarily be relevant to all trans* people. These three separate concepts are importantly experienced in interconnection with the ways in which other aspects of identity, such as sexuality, class, and race, intersect.

As gender and transgender increasingly become shorthand for discussing all of these considerations combined, distinctions are more difficult to peel apart. This conflation of multiple concepts makes understanding the varied self-understandings and experiences of different trans* people considerably more challenging and prone to erroneous comparison and categorization. Even in the most complex and insightful examinations of sex, sex category, and gender, theorists' use of "gender identity" as a unifying identification underlying all three concepts makes it difficult to understand these separate, but inter-related, aspects of one's identity.

The Problem of Binary Conflation: Gay Man or Trans* Woman?

While providing an important perspective on the development of identity labels and the evolution of language, David Valentine's (2007) *Imagining Transgender: An Ethnography of a Category* is instructive about the challenges inherent in discussing gender and sexuality without attending to the distinctions of sex, sex category, and gender, or the possibility of non-binary sex. A fundamental question that Valentine (2007) problematized throughout the text was whether a person was gay or transgender. Implicit in the text and based on which participants were being asked was that the question was actually whether or not a person was a gay *man* or a transgender *woman*. Seemingly a straightforward question on the surface, Valentine (2007) pointed out the complicated nature of the question:

> Anita claims a number of different identities: gay, drag queen, man. While she did not claim to be a transsexual or a woman, she did not dispute my characterization of her as "living as a woman" and noted that she does "everything like a woman." In other words, being on hormones and living as a woman did not make her either transexual or a woman. But later in the interview, she said:

"I don't wanna go back to a man, you know," implying that even if she is not a woman, she is no longer a man, despite her earlier assertion that "I know I'm a man."

(115)

While Valentine (2007) endeavored to complicate the question and discussed "male-bodied" people, seemingly by measure of genitalia alone, the investigation attended only to distinctions between a particular conceptualization of gender and sexual orientation. It did not address how sexual orientation was constructed in the United States nor did it differentiate sex, sex category, and gender as West and Zimmerman (1987) explicitly advised.

There are three significant errors in the question itself. First, woman and man are neither categories of gender (femininity/ masculinity) nor categories of sex (female/male), but rather a combination of the two binaries in which femininity and female together form woman, and masculinity and male form man. All other combinations require modifiers such as masculine woman, which is a gender modifier, or transsexual woman, which is a sex modifier (Seeber 2013). Is the question of whether individuals are transgender or gay asking about the sex of bodies or the gender of behaviors? Or is the question assuming that sex and gender will, or should, match up?

Second, if the question is based on the sex of bodies (as appears most likely), what is being counted as part of sex here? Are we talking about genitalia (penis or vulva)? One's perceived sex category based on secondary sex characteristics (breasts or beard)? Or are both genitalia and secondary characteristics being included, with the assumption that the two match? If the question specified whether sex or sex category were the basis for designation, the question would become less complicated as it would not assume that sex (at least as defined by genitalia) and sex category (as defined by visible secondary sex characteristics) matched. The question is problematic in the sense that whether one is a transgender woman or not is more likely a question about perceived sex category (breasts) while gay man is more likely a question of genital sex (penis). Another way to think about this is that *if both genitalia and secondary sex characteristics are counted as part of sex, it makes sense that the question cannot be answered in a straightforward manner precisely because the person being questioned does not have a binary sex*—having both breasts and a penis, for example.

Third, and related to the issue of non-binary sex or distinguishing between sex and sex category, Valentine (2007) did not address the rules for categorizing sexuality. In popular definitions, sexuality is defined by the sex/gender (generally assumed to be both binary and matching) of the individual and the sex/gender of the individual's person of desire. However, the categorization method leading to a designation of heterosexual, homosexual, or bisexual[14] is not concerned with whether the individual or person of desire are feminine or masculine (gender), rather it is concerned with whether the individual and person of desire are female or male (sex). Furthermore, this categorization requires that both individuals have a binary sex—that is, female or male, not some other category like intersex by design. How exactly does a person with a non-binary sex (breasts and a penis, or male chest and a vulva) categorize their sexuality within these constraints? If a person is neither/both male and female, what counts as the "opposite" sex?

Even if Valentine's (2007) question is modified to ask, "Is the individual a transgender female or gay male," this question still relies on having a binary sex, or a binary sex identity. This involves a perception of oneself as either female or male, not some other possible understanding of the sex of one's body. If an individual's genitalia do not match with secondary sex characteristics (a penis and breasts, for example), the individual would have to think about the body in a way that is binary in order to categorize sexuality in the "same-sex"/"opposite sex," gay/straight categorization system in order to answer (Seeber

2013). As such, someone with breasts and a penis who does not define themselves as wholly female or male may easily identify as *both* a female by sex category (transgender female, having breasts) and as a male by sexual orientation (gay male, having a penis). This is because in daily interaction people perceive the individual as female using sex category to categorize, but in sexual interaction, existing genitalia may become the means for categorization and having a penis then means defining sexuality from the position of being male.

This lack of distinction between sex, sex category, and gender and/or an inability to contemplate non-binary sex pervades much of the trans* literature, within which Valentine is only one example where a distinction would be useful. Valentine is a particularly poignant example precisely because the distinction is fundamental to an explicit and significant question of his research project. For many texts, this lack of distinction comes from the aforementioned poststructuralist/queer theory perspective's reduction of the body to gender through assertions about how "'the' body is invariably transformed into his body or her body, the body is only known through its gendered appearance" (Butler 1988: 523). For other texts, this originates in a sociological interactional/accountability approach that focuses on gender at the expense of bodies because the individuals under investigation seek sex and gender congruency (Seeber 2013). These distinctions between sex, sex category, and gender, as well as thinking about the possibility of non-binary sex become important when thinking about how and why a trans* identity continues to create challenges for trans* people long after initial transition. All people seek to have their identities confirmed by others in the process of identity verification, and these distinctions are integral to understanding how the identity verification process is being disrupted. Is the issue about behaviors (gender identity) aligning with what others expect on the basis of how they perceive the trans* person's sex category? Or is it about bodies (sex identity) being able to fit in a binary category?

Still, though Valentine (2007) did not break down and discuss distinctions around sex, sex category, and gender, he provided an insightful understanding of the creation, evolution, transmission, and uptake of language and identity categories. Language, and identity labels in particular, are created and transmitted through community groups. Thus, the definition and meaning of a label has much to do with whom one learned it from, as well as whether it is a term one learns and then uses at all. Because the United States remains highly segregated by race and class, among other simultaneously held identities, the adoption, transformation, and transmission of identity categories happens in a segregated fashion. So, while in some communities distinctions are clarified between sexual desire and sex/gender identity using labels of gay and transgender, in other communities distinctions are made using different language like femme, butch, and realness. "Gay" and "transgender" became largely disconnected concepts in White, middle and upper middle class spaces. However, in the almost exclusively working-class spaces inhabited by Blacks and dark-skinned Latino sex, gender, and sexuality minority individuals,[15] walking in "ball house categories"[16] of realness, butch, or femme, were distinctions all housed under one roof (Valentine 2007). The different social locations and understandings upheld by communities formed in the context of racial and class segregation in the United States then are important sites for exploring differences in processes of identity categorization and identity management, even beyond the distinctions in language presented here.

For the purposes of clarity, it is imperative to avoid the use of the categories woman and man and to specify whether gender (femininity/masculinity/genderqueer/other) or sex (female/male/intersex/other) is being discussed using the categorizations specific to one or the other. The necessity of this distinction becomes clear when discussing embodied capital, meaning the forms of power the body can provide an individual. This is particularly important in part because it makes a difference in the challenges people face as a result of their trans* identity becoming known and the effects these challenges have based on what sex and gender identities feel authentic to them. Are difficulties the result of the physical attributes of the body (secondary sex characteristics in particular) used to categorize a person's sex category (as male, female, or unable to categorize as binary) or based on the performance of gender—meaning masculinity and/or femininity? Or are challenges the result of how sex and gender are being combined, such as female and masculinity or male and **gender non-binary**?[17] I discuss these challenges and their relationship to authenticity as part of gender congruence capital in Chapter Two.

The distinctions between sex, sex category, and gender are additionally important because, as I documented in previous research (Seeber 2013), an individual's gender identity (desires regarding masculinity and/or femininity) may have little connection to their sex identity (body in terms of male and/or female, etc.). Someone may have been assigned male at birth, have a self-image as female, but not necessarily be interested in being female *and feminine*. In addition, gender performance will only get a person so far in terms of being sex categorized the way they would like to be. For example, long hair, makeup, and a dress may get someone who was assigned male at birth's sex category called into question and may even mean being attributed as female in some locations and under some circumstances. However, it is unlikely that the performance of femininity alone—without bodily modifications—will mean being viewed as legitimately female 100 percent of the time, at least after puberty. The effects of **testosterone** on the developing body are difficult to overcome without medical modifications to the body itself.

The idea that gender performance alone will not gain an individual assigned male at birth the sex categorization of female they wish (or vice versa) is supported by the writing of Betsy Lucal (1999). Lucal wrote of, "her experiences as a woman whose appearance often leads to gender misattribution," and again, of her, "experiences as a woman who often is mistaken as a man" (781–782). Given the discussion about the problems of using the categories man and woman, Lucal's statements require a bit of interpretation. Lucal had not made any modifications to the sex characteristics of her body, though some, like breasts, might have been less visible due to oversized, comfortable, masculine clothing. It was her performance of masculinity then that "often leads to gender misattribution" (781). By "gender" misattribution, Lucal was referring to being perceived as a man. Being viewed as a man is not just referring to being viewed as masculine, but also as *male*. This can be inferred from Lucal's descriptions of difficulties in public restrooms as it is not masculine females, but *men* (meaning males) to which bathroom users were objecting. While Lucal frequently experienced being mis-identified—enough to develop avoidance and situational management strategies—she did not always experience this type of misattribution. Masculinity alone did not result in Lucal being perceived as male 100 percent of the time. At times, she was viewed as an inappropriately gendered (masculine) female rather than as an appropriately gendered (masculine) male.

Indeed, participants in my research (Seeber 2013) pointed out that gender performance was much more stereotypically binary regardless of the person's identification as masculine, feminine, or some variation of these prior to body modifications, in an attempt to overcompensate for the ways their bodies were being perceived. Once the body had been modified to be viewed as the sex category desired, the strict performance of an "appropriate" gender became less necessary because the individual was no longer feeling the need to cover possible betrayals of the body with gender performance—masculinity was no longer necessary to prevent being viewed as "not male." For example, Jim was 24 years old, identified as racially/ethnically mixed, had started testosterone three months before being interviewed, and identified his sex as mixed. Jim discussed his resistance to societal gender expectations, but also explained that his ability to behave as he wished was also somewhat tied to his desire to have his body perceived as he wanted. He viewed the somewhat more conforming behavior as temporary, only being important until his sex category became stable. Jim explained:

> I like to talk about weights and body hair and some sports you know, so that seems very macho to me. But I also have very . . . before I was very ambiguous . . . and I like to be kind of flamboyant . . . But now it seems like I feel like I'm stifling kind of those tendencies just so I can **pass**[18] a little bit more . . . and so I feel as I get more into my transition I'll be more comfortable in doing things that aren't necessarily masculine or macho and stuff like that, but I think that's typical.

In this fashion, a person might behave, dress, and style himself in a strictly masculine way until testosterone (commonly referred to by trans* males as T) and chest surgery or **chest binding** caused others to attribute him as male 100 percent of the time. At that point in physical transition, an individual who did not identify as strictly masculine may feel freer to express less masculine behaviors such as talking with his hands, choosing different words, and being less distant or stiff in interactions because his body would ensure that he would be read by others as male.[19]

Keeping in mind the important conceptual distinctions between sex, sex category, and gender and recognizing that sex identity and gender identity are not necessarily congruent for all trans* people, I turn next to building on these ideas in terms of theoretical importance and the lived experiences of trans* respondents. To do so, I offer a theorization of embodied capital and the very real life challenges posed by having or lacking different forms of such capital.

DISCUSSION QUESTIONS

1. Why is it important to think about an individual's race and social class positions at the same time as their sex and gender identities? How does this influence your understanding of their experiences of trans* identity?
2. In addition to race, class, sex, and gender, what other identities might trans* people hold that could significantly impact their experiences of being trans*?
3. Compare and contrast previous theories of sex and gender with the author's explanation based on bodies and behaviors. How is this framework helpful in thinking about a variety of ways in which someone may express a trans* identity? Explain.

Notes

1. Trans* is used as an inclusive term for transsexual, transgender, and sex and/or gender non-conforming people. This is becoming the more common term of inclusion. Additionally, I use this term due to the sex/gender conflation and focus on gender implied in using transgender as an umbrella term.
2. A table of basic demographic information including name, age at time of interview, race/ethnicity, income, educational attainment, and relationship status appears in Appendix B.
3. Travestí identity is first about sexuality, being the penetrated partner of a male, and second about sex and gender—female breasts, hips, and other bodily features while retaining a penis combined with feminine dress and behavior scripts.
4. Caitlyn Jenner is a former Olympian and well known television personality from the TV series "Keeping up with the Kardashians"; Chaz Bono is an actor, writer, musician, and the child of musicians Sonny Bono and Cher; Lana Wachowski is a screenwriter, director, and producer well known as co-writer and executive producer of The Matrix, along with her trans* sister, Lilly Wachowski.

5. Although scientists and doctors began writing in the late nineteenth century on precursors of trans* identities, the majority of scholarship prior to the 1990s was focused on the medicalization of transsexualism and the presumed mental pathology of trans* individuals.

6. Notable exceptions to intersectional exclusion include Valentine 2007, Cotten 2012a, and Cotten 2012b. There is also an emerging presence of memoirs written by transwomen of color (Mock 2014; Narinesingh 2012), however, an extensive search found not a single memoir written by a black or non-white Latino transman, and only one (Valerio 2006) by a transman who may be perceived as a man of color by others.

7. In 2011, the journal *Feminist Studies* published a special issue called *Race and Transgender Studies*, bringing together several articles examining the intersections of trans* and racial identities (Mantilla and Waitt 2011). However, few books or articles in trans* studies explore intersecting identities of race, class, sex, and gender in a sustained fashion.

8. These terms are used to denote people who identify with the sex and gender (respectively) assigned to them at birth and to avoid the "othering" process of only marking those who are "trans*" (Stryker 2008).

9. Identity verification is a process that everyone, not only trans*-identified people, engage in. For further explanation of this process, see Burke and Stets 2009.

10. Some mark the beginning of the Civil Rights Era from the Brown v. Board of Education of Topeka, Kansas Supreme Court Ruling in 1954. However, Kenneth Janken (n.d.) notes that struggles were already underway. An anti-lynching campaign by the National Association for the Advancement of Colored People (NAACP) began in the 1930s and the legal framework for a pathway to desegregated schools began in 1929 (Janken n.d.).

11. Similar to the phenomenon of "driving while Black," where Black people are disproportionately pulled over while driving, particularly in neighborhoods where they are not expected, male-to-female transsexuals and trans* females experience a phenomenon of what has been called "walking while transgender" (Hickey 2008). This is a situation where trans* females (who are visually not categorizable as cis* females) walking on a street, particularly at night, and especially in areas known for sex work,

are assumed to be sex workers and disproportionately detained. While this happens to White trans* females, it is more commonly an issue for trans* females of color.

12. Sometimes used to refer to performing a combination of femininity and masculinity. Also sometimes used to mean gender incongruent—masculine female or feminine male—or as a political identity to acknowledge that more than two sex/gender combinations are possible.

13. Shorthand commonly used in personal adds, W4M is an acronym for Woman looking for Man. M4W stands for Man looking for Woman.

14. There are many more possible labels for sexuality within American culture such as pansexual, omnisexual, demisexual, sapiosexual, or queer, however, mainstream categorization generally relies on a hetero/homo/bi system of categorization.

15. Latinx, pronounced "La-teen-ex," "is the gender-neutral alternative to Latino, Latina and even Latin@. Used by scholars, activists and an increasing number of journalists, Latinx is quickly gaining popularity among the general public" (Ramirez 2016).

16. Ball house categories refer to the performance categories available in a dance/drag show called a "ball," from the word ballroom. People worked on their performances and outfits and sometimes lived together in chosen family relationships called houses. For further information see Valentine 2007 or the film Paris is Burning (1991).

17. Neither (entirely) feminine nor masculine.

18. To "pass" means to be viewed by others as fitting into one of the two socially available sex categories (male or female) that one was not assigned at birth. For example, someone assigned female at birth and viewed by others as male is said to "pass" as male.

19. See also Dozier 2005.

2 Embodied Resources

It's not the general public that [tries to overturn laws protecting trans* people] or hurts you. It's one or two lone wolves and you don't know where that is going to come from. Now, I've never felt that I needed to carry a gun through anything trans* related. I've been harassed before, but I only get harassed if I am with a trans* woman who doesn't pass well. They don't focus on me; they focus on her. Or, I get harassed as a woman.

—Penny

Body capital or embodied capital refers to the ways in which the body can be used as a resource for power. Pierre Bourdieu (1984, 1997) theorized four forms of capital: economic, cultural, social, and symbolic. According to Bourdieu's theorization, cultural capital referred to assets such as education, style of speech, and dress, all of which were assets a person accumulated over time, similar to accumulating economic capital, money. Embodied capital was initially discussed by Bourdieu as a sub-form of cultural capital that comprised "long-lasting dispositions of the mind and body" (1997: 47).

While Bourdieu theorized that power accumulated through various forms of capital, he never directly addressed power attached to race and ethnicity, sex categorization, gender, or sexuality. In response, feminist and critical race theorists expanded upon Bourdieu's original ideas to include these other important forms of power. Additionally, within discourses about beauty, racism, sexism, and ableism, scholars showed the importance of certain types of bodies and the power that they hold within specific social locations (i.e. Edmonds 2010 on beauty capital and plastic surgery; Clare 2009 on ableism).

We have learned from critical race theorists and feminist sociologists on both sides of the Atlantic the important role that bodies and body parts play in the negotiation of racism, ethnic boundaries, community formation, and belonging (Adkins and Skeggs 2004; Alexander and Knowles 2005; Ali 2003; Banks 1998; Bordo 1993; Nayak 1997; Noble 2005). For example, in *A White Side of Black Britain: Interracial Intimacy and Racial Literacy* (2010), France Winddance Twine, a North American sociologist, provided an ethnography of the labor of **transracial** mothers. In this longitudinal ethnography, Twine extended the theoretical tools of Bourdieu and brought him into dialogue with critical race theorists. She did this by providing two new concepts: ethnic capital and racial literacy. Her discussion of **ethnic capital** bears directly upon the lives of trans* people negotiating embodied capital.

Twine (2010) detailed a specific form of embodied capital when analyzing what she conceptualized as ethnic capital that White (English and Irish) parents with children of African-Caribbean heritage used and helped their children, particularly daughters, achieve. Through practices such as hair care and heritage cooking, White mothers contributed to the achievement of Black identification and ethnic capital within the Black community by developing tastes and consumption practices in line with Black ethnic identity. To gain respect and be viewed as culturally competent by their Black family members, transracial mothers and multiracial daughters participated in hair care regimens that include seeking out the services of Black women in salons devoted to the maintenance of Black women's hair.

In Twine's theoretical framework, hair care constituted a form of ethnic capital that was neglected by Bourdieu. It was a form of embodied capital as it involved the use of bodily assets, but was also a matter of cultural performance. Quoting the earlier work of Kobena Mercer, a Black British cultural theorist, Twine wrote:

> As organic matter produced by physiological processes, human hair seems to be a natural aspect of the body. Yet hair is never a straightforward, biological fact, because it is almost always groomed, prepared, cut, concealed and generally worked upon by human hands. Such practices socialize hair, making it the medium of significant statements about self, society and the codes of value that bind them, or do not. In this way hair is merely raw material, constantly processed by cultural practices which thus invest it with meanings and value.
>
> (Twine 2010: 156)

Within Black community spaces, evidence of hair care regimens that were considered appropriate for Black women, such as braids, provided the wearer (and her caretakers) with respect and esteem—power—that otherwise would not have accrued.

Further expanding on the idea of capital, I discuss here two different forms of embodied capital that are particularly important in examining and comparing the experiences of trans* people. First, how do "congruent" or "incongruent" sex and gender affect what daily challenges a trans* person faces? If others view a person as female, is their performance of gender (femininity) deemed appropriate? I explore the embodied capital of "gender congruence," written *on* the body, to address these questions. This form of capital is clearly viewed by scholars in the humanities and social sciences alike as a performed and achieved form of capital (i.e. Butler 1988, 1990, 1993; Fausto-Sterling 2000; Fenstermaker and West 2002; West and

Zimmerman 1987). Second, what does it mean experientially to be able to be categorized as either male or female as opposed to others having difficulty fitting you into one of these two boxes? Often discussed in terms of "passing,"[1] I examine the embodied capital of sex category. This form of capital is based *in* bodily characteristics controlled by hormones and requires surgical intervention to otherwise "achieve." It is also more difficult to categorize as performative on the same level as gender. For example, Chris Shilling, a sociologist of the body, noted that the body was increasingly becoming a body "*project* which should be worked at and accomplished as part of an *individual's* self-identity" (2003: 4, emphasis in original). Shilling had also long suggested that the body be considered as a form of capital all its own, rather than subsumed under cultural capital (1991). In this context it is increasingly important to extend Bourdieu's (1984, 1997) ideas on capital that is embodied. Finally, I discuss the power associated with these versions of embodied capital.

Embodied Capital and Gender Congruence

Each and every one of us is at all times performing gender. Some people perform it "appropriately" according to the conventional rules of their society, meaning males performing the current conceptualization of masculinity and females performing femininity (Butler 1988; West and Zimmerman 1987). As scholars such as West and Zimmerman (1987) pointed out, in addition to performing gender, we are constantly being judged on our performance in accordance with the expectations of the society around us. Like the ethnic capital discussed by Twine (2010), those who perform to expectations, for example people who are visibly female and perform appropriate femininity with acceptable hair styles, make up, feminine posture and etiquette, etc., are judged as culturally competent people.

Those who transgress the rules of gender performance, for example those perceived as female who wear a suit and tie with a masculine cut rather than a feminine cut have less gender congruence capital in most situations. Judgments about the appropriateness of gender performance are also structured in part by dominant expectations of gender as they intersect with racial, ethnic, and class hierarchies. A person viewed as female will be judged not only on femininity, but by specific beliefs, for example about Black, Latina, or White femininity (Collins 2004; Fenstermaker and West 2002) and white, blue, or pink collar femininity.

In *Just One of the Guys? Transgender Men and the Persistence of Gender Inequality*, Kristen Schilt (2010) provided an analysis of the occupational experiences of trans* men,[2] meaning individuals assigned female at birth, who no longer identified as female. She showed how trans* males may get drawn into the social networks of cis* males. However, their degree of inclusion depends on their distance from or closeness to performance of culturally dominant masculinity as well as their physical ability to be viewed as stereotypically male. Schilt noted, "Being treated as one of the guys by men . . . can bring more recognition and camaraderie, particularly for white transmen [sic] read as heterosexual" (2010: 68). Schilt also emphasized the racialized nature of masculinity in U.S. society when she stated, "Highlighting the relationality between embodiments of maleness, however, white, tall transmen [sic] who can physically pass report greater gains in [authority, respect, and recognition] than transmen [sic] who are men of color, short, and/or gender-ambiguous" (2010: 86).

A perfect example of this observation about inclusion (and privilege) afforded to gender congruent trans* males made by Schilt (2010) is a comparison of the experiences of Magic and Benji. Magic, 43 at the time of interview, identified as male, noted that others viewed him as White, and was maybe an inch short of six feet tall. Several years after transition he described his post-transition experiences of privilege:

> For example, let's say I'm in a store and there's a few people waiting to be helped and nobody really knows who's first, they'll be like, "sir, have you been helped?" And it'll be me first. I'm like, why not the Asian lady? Why not the Black man? Why not the elderly lady? Why is it me? . . . I can frame that however I want and say, well it's because I'm a man, it's because I'm White, it's because I'm a White man, or it's because I'm taller than anybody . . . But I can just feel . . . I have a sense that it's White male privilege. Like I'm walking on the sidewalk, people move out of the way. Not because I'm like 295 pounds and big, but because I'm a White guy.

In striking contrast, Benji, a 54-year-old trans* male, identified as multiracial White and Filipino, and was 5'2" tall. He found that his height was a significant impediment to any gains in sex category-based privilege. He explained:

> I think that any maybe gain that I might have had, what they call male privilege, from transitioning has been just about wiped out by being a very short man. If you listen to the media, they promote this heightism thing. I don't know, but they constantly joke about short men. I can't even tell you how many jokes I've heard about Ryan Seacrest being short and Tom Cruise being short. They tower over me. For me to keep hearing this message, it impacts a lot of things . . . For example in class, I am the guy who asks the most questions in class. I try to give the professors everything they're looking for. I try to be a model student. When I'm at work, I try to demonstrate to the boss that I'm innovative, that I can think outside the box. I go out of my way to prove to people that I'm

worthy and I know that part of it is compensating for the fact that they don't just look at me and say we trust that you can do what you . . . You have to prove it.

The average height for White males in the United States is 5'10", which made Magic, at 5'11" taller than the average White male and Benji at 5'2" significantly shorter than average (Fryar et al. 2016). However, Benji's height was much closer to the average 5'5" for Filipino males (Roser 2016). Because he was viewed as Asian American and was shorter, Benji did not fit the stereotypical image of the dominant male in a U.S. context—an image that includes the characteristics White and tall. As a result, Benji accrued less gender congruence capital (in addition to male privilege) because he less physically matched the expectations of male than Magic, who was both White and tall. Thus, no matter how well Benji performed masculinity, he was still farther from the culturally dominant combination of maleness and masculinity required to best accrue the capital of gender congruence.

People who may fall under the trans* umbrella such as gender non-conforming and genderqueer individuals accrue far less embodied capital of gender congruence, facing more challenges as a result. These individuals likely view the lack of gender congruence capital as less important than living their authentic sense of gendered self. However, for trans* people who identify in a more binary, gender conforming fashion, the lack of gender congruence capital is likely viewed as a loss, particularly when it is not their gender performance that causes the loss of capital. These individuals may be performing masculinity or femininity in a historically and culturally appropriate way for the society they live in and still have that performance harshly judged because their bodies are still betraying them. If an individual assigned male at birth is still visually appearing male to others then their performance of femininity, no matter how well accomplished, will be viewed as the incorrect gender performance because it is still not congruent with how others perceive their sex category. Thus, less gender congruence capital accrues, even when gender is being performed well, which results in more challenges to being recognized by others as one wishes to be seen.

Both gender non-conforming/genderqueer and gender conforming, but "non-passing" trans* people lack the embodied capital of gender congruence. However, the effects of this lack of capital are very different for those who feel authentic as non-conforming in comparison to those who feel authentic conforming, but are simply not able to "pass." For the gender non-conforming/genderqueer it may simply be the price for living an authentic sense of self in a world that continues to insist that females be feminine and males be masculine. Lack of embodied capital is an unfortunate circumstance for the gender non-conforming/genderqueer, but perhaps it is a lack that can be repaired by educating others about how femininity and masculinity, as well as their links to female and male bodies, are socially constructed expectations and not biological facts. However, for those trans*-identified individuals who are performing gender in culturally appropriate ways for the sex category they wish to be seen as, but whose bodies still cause them to be viewed in a different sex category, this lack of embodied capital is a constant reminder that their bodies are still betraying them in achieving their authentic sense of self.

This combination of wrong sex category plus right gender performance results in a loss of gender congruence capital, but it also points to a deeper form of embodied capital based in the sex category attribution of others and "passing." For individuals assigned female at birth who identify as male and masculine, being sex categorized by others as female may only lead to a loss of gender congruence capital if the performance of masculinity is extreme. Our society maintains more leeway in what were once considered masculine behaviors for female bodies (short hair, wearing pants, occupational pursuits) than for feminine behaviors for male bodies (makeup, dresses, skirts, high heels nurturing). As a result, when an individual was assigned male at birth and is still sex categorized as male by others, but views herself as female and feminine, she may experience *both* a loss of gender congruence capital as well as sex category capital. This occurs because people may begin to question the sex category of an individual assigned male at birth and who is so clearly performing femininity. In contrast, except in performances of extreme masculinity, those assigned female at birth are unlikely to have their sex categorization called into question based on gender performance because more gender flexibility is allowed for female-categorized people.

Sex Category Attribution and "Passing"

Twine (2010) refered to ethnic capital as something "written on the body." In a similar fashion, the embodied capital of gender congruence is written on the body. People may use parts of the body such as hair and make it social through styling, or may emphasize different parts of the body with clothing cut to highlight some areas and mask others. Individuals may also act in ways socially attributed to one type of body and not to others such as talking while gesturing with the hands and choosing gendered language, such as topless versus shirtless. When it comes to sex category attribution and embodied capital, we shift from talking about things written on the body to things written *in* the body. In this case, bodily attributes that are visible and available to make use of for sex categorizing someone are the medium of capital, not the social aspects of or associations with these characteristics. For example, the presence of an Adam's apple will likely evoke social expectations regarding masculinity (gender), but *first* it is used to mark an individual as male. This distinction is important if for no other reason than because in order to assess someone's gender performance as appropriate or not, we must have a sex category to compare it with. If a person is performing femininity, we can only judge that performance as congruent and "correct" or not if we are first able to attribute the person as male or female.

People become uncomfortable and uncertain about how to interact with an individual if the person's sex category and gender performance do not "match" in the socially expected combination of male-masculine or female-feminine. This discomfort causes the loss of gender congruence capital. But what if someone cannot determine what an individual's sex category is in the first place, let alone whether or not it "matches" with gender performance? Not only do people become uncomfortable and uncertain about how to act, interaction begins to revolve around trying to figure out how to sex categorize the individual so that mundane social interaction may resume. Readers might recall the infamous character Pat from *Saturday Night Live* (SNL) in the 1990s. In an interview in *Salon* (Bolonik 2015) Julia Sweeney, creator of Pat, made clear that Pat was not trans*-identified, but the predicament of others interacting with Pat is instructive for thinking through this type of embodied capital for trans* and cis* people alike.

Although Pat was discussed as being ambiguously gendered—not clearly performing masculinity or femininity in terms of clothing, posture, word choice, hairstyle, etc.—Pat was also portrayed in a way that made sex categorization difficult if not impossible. Pat's weight made it impossible to tell if Pat's chest was male or female. The pants Pat wore did nothing to help identify what genitalia might be covered. Pat did not have a beard or a visible beard shadow to rule out that Pat was female, but this also did not necessarily rule out being male as not all males have signs of facial hair growth. A search through the SNL archives[3] showed how a variety of interactions were disrupted by people's inability to sex categorize Pat or assess what version of gender to use as appropriate.[4]

Scholars have pointed out that many of the characteristics we use to categorize someone as male or female occur with great variety within a category and with a good deal of overlap across categories. These characteristics are then individually ineffective at determining males from females as noted at the beginning of this chapter.[5] For example, females vary in height, as do males; some females are taller than some males, and most of us are within the range of height where males and females overlap. However, as I pointed out previously (Seeber 2013), we use more than one characteristic at the same time to decide whether we view someone as male or female, and very few people fall within the male-female overlap on *enough* characteristics to make categorizing them as difficult as it was with Pat. In fact, part of the reason that the inability to sex categorize Pat was so disruptive to interaction was precisely because this inability happens so rarely.

Rare as it may otherwise be, trans* people who medically modify the sex characteristics of their bodies often move through a period of being uncategorizable or end up in a permanent state of unknown sex-category. One of the fascinating things about attending a trans* conference is that asking what pronouns someone uses (he, she, their, hir, etc.) is not only accepted as proper etiquette, but often a necessity precisely because people attending identify in a variety of ways in terms of sex and gender. They may also be at various stages of physical transition. So if you meet someone who could be male, but also might be female, and is combining masculine and feminine gender, there is no way to know without asking directly how they identify. Is this an individual who is moving from one place on the sex and/or gender spectrum to another? Which direction might they be moving? Or is "both/neither" male and female, masculine and feminine how they identify?

While in the context of a trans* conference this ambiguity is expected, accepted, or even celebrated, in daily life appearing in such a way that others cannot categorize you easily as male or female presents a host of problems. Logistical problems arise, such as if I ask where the bathroom is or where the fitting rooms are at a store: where does the employee direct me? In addition, many people respond to discomfort by excluding those who appear to initiate the anxiety, or by acting out against them. As I have already mentioned, the distress onlookers are responding to in such instances is not about whether a person is performing gender in the way expected by society. Rather, the individual cannot be identified as either female or male, and so there is nothing for the viewer to compare the performance of masculinity or femininity to in order to determine the appropriateness of gender in the first place. This difficulty with sex categorization—let alone gender congruence—is further complicated by evidence that suggests people have difficulty with cross-racial identification, which is an issue I examine further in discussing sex category capital and transition direction later in the chapter (Ackerman et al. 2006; Brigham and Barkowitz 1978; Smith, Stinson, and Prosser 2004).

The ability to attribute a binary (male or female) sex category to someone is a deeper issue than judgments about gender. Individual trans* people may identify their own sex category in a variety of binary or non-binary ways including male, female, intersex, not-female, not-male, etc. Additionally, a trans* person may not view "passing" as the binary sex category they were not assigned at birth as their goal. However, an individual's self-identification and goals about how others will categorize them are not really relevant to having sex category capital or not. What matters in terms of power, challenges faced in daily life, and what resources a person has to manage challenges in life is whether or not the individual is viewed by others as fitting within the binary system of sex categorization. For instance, it does not matter whether I identify as male or not. Because I am easily viewed by others as male—as opposed to a non-binary sex category or otherwise visually trans*—I, at least superficially, can blend into society and face fewer daily challenges to my identity than someone who is noticeably trans*, ambiguously sexed, or suspected to be trans* by others. While there are situations in which my trans* identity will be disclosed whether I want it to or not, in day-to-day life I generally get to be in charge of whether my identity as trans* becomes known because I am viewed by others as male.

Sex Category and Age at Transition

Two issues arise when talking about sex category embodied capital—age and, for transsexual people, the sex category one is moving to. Everyone has heard someone ask, and has probably been the questioner at some point asking, "Is it a boy or a girl?" In asking this question the interest is not about whether or not the child identifies with or performs masculinity or femininity. The interest is in whether the child is male or female and observers will judge masculinity or femininity on the basis of the sex category of the child. Before puberty there are few or no visible physical markers of sex category in day-to-day life. Voices are pitched pretty much the same, no one is growing facial hair, and almost everyone is flat chested. Hairstyle, clothing, and other chosen gender markers are the materials commonly used for sex category attribution. At the onset of puberty, however, hormones significantly affect the visual markings of the body; the longer those hormones have had to work their magic, the more difficult those bodily signs are to overcome should one wish to change categories.

In addition to the difficulties of masking years of hormonal effects on the body, the earlier someone starts hormone replacement therapy, the more time the new hormones have to work *their* magic. Given the effects of higher levels of **estrogens** or **androgens** over time, the earlier someone starts hormonal transition the less likely they will continue to be suspected to be trans* or sex categorized according to the sex category assigned at birth. The conundrum presented by the effectiveness of hormones based on age at the start of replacement therapy and concerns about when it is appropriate to begin hormone treatment has been debated in the medical care of trans* people for years. Research has shown that some trans* people identify as a sex category they were not assigned at birth as early as age seven (Rahilly 2015) and perhaps even earlier. Some people in this study indicated they knew they were different by the age of four or five. However, difficult as it may be for society to accept transition in adults, providing hormone replacement therapy to a seven-year-old seems out of the question in our current social climate, in part because of the relative permanency of hormone treatment. For this reason, hormone blockers are sometimes used for youth who clearly self-identify as trans* and are discussed in the **Standards of Care** for the Health of Transsexual, Transgender, and Gender-Nonconforming People guidelines produced by The World Professional Association for Transgender Health, also known as WPATH (2012). Even the use of hormone blockers, though, remains controversial in spite of the fact that earlier treatment would provide higher sex category embodied capital.

Examining the lives of Leddy and Donna illuminated the profound difference that age at transition made in sex category embodied capital. Leddy, a 45-year-old, White trans* female, knew she was different from an early age. Although she was unable to label the difference until much later she said, "I grew up and it just really felt awkward my whole life." After finishing high school and then vocational school, Leddy landed a job with good pay. During that time, she had also met a few trans* people and was therefore able to put a name to the difference she had long felt. A few years on the job was enough for her to save the money and make the decision that she needed to transition. In the early 1990s, while in her early 20s, Leddy recalled, "I had my surgery and it was one of those marathon type surgeries that they pretty much did everything all in one day. I was in the operating room for 16 hours I think."

I met Leddy in front of an antique motorcycle shop in a mid-sized city in the South. Leddy and I had corresponded only by email and because her name is gender-neutral-to-masculine, I had incorrectly assumed that she would be a trans* male. I later noted that when I pulled up in front of the shop:

> I rolled down my window to ask a woman standing in the parking lot if it was ok to park there since it was after business hours and she said I was fine. I got out of the car, searched through my email on my phone to find my interviewee's phone number and was surprised when calling that the woman turned around holding her phone—she was the person I was looking for. From the name she had given, I was expecting a trans* man and thus was thoroughly confused at how this person could be 5 years into transition up until I started the interview and asked about pronouns and identity and she started telling me her background story.

Leddy visually appeared so clearly female that I would never have imagined she was a trans* female, and because of the name she had given me, I was expecting that 5 years into transition a trans* male would have looked at least somewhat male. Leddy even retained sex category capital without maintaining strictly feminine gender congruence capital—with her short hair, comfy t-shirt and sweatshirt, she looked very much at home in the "grease-monkey" setting of the shop. Given her female embodiment there was no need to be particularly feminine to ensure categorization as female.

In contrast to Leddy, Donna had less embodied capital as female. Donna, White and 63 when we spoke, also transitioned in the early 1990s, but was in her early 40s as opposed to Leddy who had been in her early 20s. Donna was married for 20 years before transitioning, and although her wife had known about her trans* identity for 18 of those 20 years, Donna said her ex-wife, "made my life very miserable." Donna lost a very well-paying job when the company she worked for closed down, which added significant strain to her life. At that point, Donna and her wife separated and Donna began to dress in a feminine fashion and started taking hormones. After a couple of years of living "half and half," as she called it, Donna moved to a new city and started living full time as female and feminine. When I met Donna at her apartment she was wearing dark blue jeans and a long-sleeved black blouse with dark red flowers on it. She had her long hair braided with feathers at the ends of the braids in Native American fashion. I noted that, "she has strong, but not so much male looking hands."[6] I also documented that she sees herself as "mostly passable." As with those who have yet to reach puberty, sex category is less distinguishable with those who are older, and Donna's age helped her look more grandmotherly rather than sex category ambiguous.

In comparison to Leddy, Donna was dressed and had her hair styled in a more stereotypically feminine fashion. However, I recognized Donna as trans* whereas I was confused that Leddy was the individual I had shown up to interview. Donna pointed out that her visibility as trans* extended beyond my perception and that she had spent about 5 years working on the pitch of her voice and learning "how to articulate in a more feminine manner." She explained that she learned to use fewer contractions, made fewer personal, or "I" statements, and asked many, many more questions. This added work on femininity was required in order to make up for the lower sex category capital Donna had because, as she noted, "When I talked, people knew" that she was trans*. It was true that Leddy had undergone more surgery than Donna. However, the difference in sex category capital had little to do with surgeries and more to do with the age when they started hormone replacement. This was because neither of them had facial feminization surgeries beyond the tracheal shave Leddy had to reduce the size of her Adam's apple. The most visible difference between the two could be described as a softness. Leddy's skin appeared less weathered and worn than Donna's in a way that, rather than simply age, suggested the longer presence of testosterone for Donna.

Sex Category and Transition Direction

The second consideration in sex category embodied capital is the sex category to which someone is moving. There are two reasons why where someone started and where they are going makes a significant difference. The first reason is due to the social practice of assigning sex category to people in our daily lives within a patriarchal society. Sex category attribution operates on an "if can" assumption: if the person can be categorized as male, then do so; if the person cannot be categorized as male, but can be categorized as female, then do so; if the person cannot be categorized as male and cannot be categorized as female, scrutinize more carefully until an attribution can be made. Since the default categorization under patriarchy is male, it is typically easier for those moving from female to male to be identified as male than for those moving from male to female to be identified as female (Kessler and McKenna 1978; Schilt 2010; West and Zimmerman 1987). This trend is strengthened in particular for those who are dark-skinned Black or Latinx when being perceived by White observers. When White observers fail to pick up on distinctions as cross-racial identification, research has suggested the "ambiguity" for the White observer is even more likely to lead to an attribution of male (Ackerman et al. 2006; Brigham and Barkowitz 1978; Smith, Stinson, and Prosser 2004).

The second reason that a person's birth assigned and desired sex categories make a difference has to do with the temporary and permanent effects of androgens such as testosterone, and estrogens (Schilt 2010). For example, once the voice has deepened, no amount of estrogen will make it higher because a permanent thickening of the vocal chords causes the deepening of the voice. Similarly, facial hair growth cannot be reversed and is a sufficient characteristic itself for male sex category attribution. Shaving and makeup will work to a point for trans* females, but electrolysis or laser hair removal are usually required. Estrogens will cause a softening of the skin, but the longer androgens have had to roughen the look of the skin, the more difficult this effect becomes to reverse—as Donna's difficulty with sex category capital demonstrated. As such, it is much easier to go from softer to rougher skin appearance than the opposite direction. Height, also significantly affected by the balance of androgens and estrogens, creates additional difficulties for trans* people. While both are difficult, it is still easier to be categorized as male and draw less sex category scrutiny as a shorter than average male than to be categorized as a female if a person is significantly taller than most females. Comparing the realities of Zoe and David's lives highlighted the difference in experiences based on the direction of sex category transition.

Zoe, a 52-year-old White trans* female, started hormone replacement therapy in 2004 at the age of 43 and legally adopted her feminine name in 2005. Zoe was 6' tall, thin, with an angular face and deep voice. When we met she was wearing a shoulder-length, light brown wig, had her makeup done in a casual, natural looking fashion, and had bright pink polish on the nails of her slender, long fingers. She was casually dressed in light blue jeans with a long-sleeved, black, women's cut t-shirt. I had the pleasure of meeting Zoe with her wife Chris. The two were similarly dressed in a casually feminine style of t-shirts and jeans. Feeling close to them after a long interview and through more casual conversation, I made plans to meet up with them for an outing the following day to tour around the rural area where Zoe and Chris had been born, raised, and lived nearly their entire lives. The morning of the outing Zoe was again casually dressed in jeans and a long-sleeved t-shirt, but in her more common going out fashion—without makeup or wig.

her own naturally long hair showed, thinning in the front, which created the impression of a high forehead and made her strong brow ridge more prominent.

Early in the interview Chris pointed out that Zoe had long legs in a way that highlighted this quality as enviable for feminine females, but at 6', Zoe's overall height certainly contributed to the fact that she was not always viewed as female. Shy in many situations, Zoe's voice was also likely to cause suspicion over the phone or when she spoke up in public. But mostly, her face lacked the soft roundness of her wife's and was the most telling of her history as male. When out and about with her wife in situations where their names were on paper (opening a bank account, adding one to the other's insurance, etc.), the misrecognition was telling. Because her wife's name was more masculine sounding than her own, Zoe was often mistaken as Chris and Chris, being visually more female, was assumed to be Zoe. I admit, having corresponded over email with Chris to set up the interview, I was curious before even meeting them how this played out. Both have a wonderful sense of humor and enjoyed the confusion this created. As Zoe commented of one such situation of misrecognition, "We milked that one!"

In contrast to Zoe, David had no trouble being viewed as male in daily life. David, a 49-year-old White trans* male, also began transition in 2004 at the age of 40—almost the exact same time and age as Zoe. He started hormones, then 2 years later had **chest reconstruction** and a complete **hysterectomy** all in one surgery. Next, he changed his name and "gender"[7] on all of his legal documentation. Just a few months before I met him, David started a series of genital surgeries and had a couple left to go. David's voice was soft, but not really feminine. At our interview he was comfortably dressed in a long-sleeved blue shirt, blue jeans, and indoor/outdoor tan slippers. He had short, light brown hair, thinning a little near the front, and wore glasses. Other pictures I found online showed him in a smart power suit with a well-groomed mustache and beard.

Although David was not particularly tall, he was within the range of average male height—probably around 5'6"–5'8". Even if he were shorter, however, given the slight thinning of his hairline at the front, and especially the presence of his facial hair, it was unlikely anyone would ever guess he was anything but male his entire life. In addition to the roughening of the skin caused by testosterone, the presence of facial hair gave David, and most whom transition from female to male, a rougher facial presentation. The lack of a prominent Adam's apple was unnoticeable, especially with the presence of facial hair. So even though Zoe and David transitioned in the same year and at nearly the same age in their lives, at about 10 years after the start of transition, David was less likely to have his sex category questioned than Zoe. This difference in sex category recognition was because of the direction of transition and the effects of this on how their bodies were visually perceived by others.

Notably, Zoe and David were both White and, compared to Black, Latinx, and other trans* individuals who are not qualified for whiteness, they were far less likely to endure the level of surveillance trans* people of color endure. Racially-based patterns of surveillance are likely to translate into more scrutiny for dark-skinned Black and Latino trans* males. This would theoretically lead to less sex category capital for them because of the increased possibility that surveillance may lead to questioning of their sex category. However, if the person surveilling is White, difficulties in cross-racial perception combined with male as the default assumption in patriarchal society mean that even dark-skinned Black and Latino trans* males are less likely to have their sex category called into question than trans* females, except within same-race interactions.

The Power of Embodied Capital

The power of embodied capital was visible across a variety of life domains, including areas of challenges such as family, work, and health care as discussed in the chapters to come. As noted previously, some individuals performed the expected gender of the sex category they wish to be considered, but because their bodies were still viewed as the sex category they were assigned at birth, they continued to be judged as inappropriately performing gender. Those who did get viewed as the binary sex category they wished to be seen as benefited from sex category embodied capital, often whether or not they were judged as appropriately performing gender. As I pointed out, Leddy's bodily appearance was so clearly female that her lack of performing femininity was irrelevant to her sex category capital. Since Donna and Zoe identified as female, but were not always recognized as female by others, they had to deal more openly with what I have called the paradox of (trans*)identity—knowing sex and gender are changeable in a world that believes sex and gender to be dichotomous and unchanging throughout our lives. They visually disrupted the belief of dichotomous, static sex and gender for others with whom they came into contact. In addition to this effect of a loss of sex category capital, even though Donna and Zoe performed femininity, because their performance was *not* being judged against female sex category, they also often lost the embodied capital, or positive assessment, of gender congruence. While Donna and Zoe were both White and working-class, others like Monique and Maya (introduced in Chapter 4 and Chapter 5 respectively) simultaneously risked loss of embodied capital in a U.S. context based on racial discrimination against their dark Black skin.

The importance of the distinction between gender and sex category becomes visible when discussing the challenges different trans* people do or do not face and how they can manage things that arise. For example, I still have the embodied capital of sex categorization even though most people assume from my version of masculinity and femininity (intentional gender nonconformity) that I am a gay male, which may limit my embodied capital of gender congruence. Being viewed as male is an example of others failing to verify my identity (Burke and Stets 2009) because people are viewing me as a sex category that I do not embrace myself. The interruption theory of stress (Burke and Stets 2009), states that this creates a low level of anxiety, which is true for me as I am constantly reminded that whether I want to be or not, others will categorize me as male or female, and male at least seems closer to "correct" for me. So although an identity verification failure in sex categorization occurs, my sex category capital allows me to at least avoid dealing openly with the paradox of (trans*)identity. Even though I know that my sex category has changed, others do not know just by seeing me that their assumptions about sex and gender being dichotomous and unchangeable are inaccurate. I do not become the focus of their confusion in day-to-day interaction and my Whiteness keeps my identity from being further scrutinized in the ways that dark-skinned bodies are scrutinized and surveilled.

In addition to avoiding daily interaction around the paradox of (trans*)identity, sex category capital has an effect on other areas of life as well. I have often heard trans* people talk about getting friends and families on board with their transition, especially insofar as using a new name and preferred pronouns, by simply letting embodied capital of sex category accrue and do the work for them. The more male their bodies became (or female if they were assigned male at birth), the more sense it made to friends and family to use correct names and pronouns. I personally experienced anxiety early in transition out in public with my family when someone referred to me as she instead of he, or used my former, very feminine name. Now that I appear entirely male, not only does it visually make more sense for family members to use male pronouns and call me Andrew or Andie, but also the anxiety has shifted from me to those who mispronoun or misname me. My mother and I have talked about how if we are out in public now and she refers to me as "she" or "my daughter" or uses my former name, she knows that it is her sanity that will be questioned rather than my identity.

There are also more mundane experiences with profound effects that occur on the basis of sex category embodied capital and people's assumptions about sex as unchangeable. For example, I have had friends, acquaintances, and people I have interviewed for several projects tell me how they got the "gender" marker[8] changed on their driver's license or other documentation simply because the worker behind the desk looked at them and assumed a mistake must have been made at some point. The identification or paperwork read female, but the individual clearly appeared male to the worker. In 2015 I finally experienced this myself since, having moved states, I was in need of a new driver's license. Although my previous state license listed me as "F," without any questions asked of me, the license I was handed to check for any errors said "M." Because I do not actually identify as male, I pointed out the error to the customer service representative and said, "legally I'm female," to which she responded "Seriously?" When I asked a question later, the representative politely answered "Yes ma'am."[9]

There are likewise challenges related to the embodied capital of gender congruence in addition to the difficulties that arise based on the ability to be sex categorized in a binary system. Trans* people have often discussed changing their behaviors in accordance with a change in how others viewed their sex category—or how they wished others viewed it—that showed an awareness of how important gender performance and the gender expectations of others were to daily life. As Donna pointed out above, she learned to change her choice of words, made few "I" statements and asked many more questions. In situations where her gender performance was being judged against a sex category that was not female, these changes did not increase her gender congruence capital. However, in instances where others did view her as female, her gender congruence capital increased because of these conscious changes to her behavior.

In a similar manner, trans* males have pointed out the importance of gender performance and expectations of others.

They have often talked about becoming aware that they were being viewed as male because of the reactions they received from people they perceived as female—reactions that let trans* males know that females were now viewing them as a threat. This reaction of fear was especially pronounced toward Black trans* males because of the stereotypes of Black males as dangerous criminals in the United States. Together, I interviewed friends Taye, a Black trans* male, and Carlos, a Latino trans* male (often viewed as White by his own account), both in their late forties. Taye talked about his difficulties with the perception of Black males as criminals, pointing out that race and class get invoked in conversations about perpetrators, but not in discussions about victims of violence. This conversation prompted Carlos to discuss the change in his thought process and behaviors regarding victims and perpetrators during the course of his transition:

> [P]rior to transition . . . I was so uncomfortable with this idea of being a victim because I was a woman. Because I was a female, I was a victim. And I was . . . so angry at that assertion that—not that I did anything consciously to be a more masculine female or to be a part of the dyke rather than lesbian community, it's just where I naturally fell . . . I think for me, part of being a dyke was basically saying, "Fuck you and your victimhood." Like, "Screw you and your poor me." Like, "I'm a lesbian and I'm a dyke, so I don't give, you know, men don't have shit over me," right? So then coming into transition with that in my brain, I feel like what do I need to do now, to not be the person walking down the street where the general assumption is, "Oh there goes a man, there goes a perpetrator of violence and power."

Eli, a 40-year-old White trans* male, echoed Carlos's concern about being viewed as a threat by females and came up with one behavioral solution. He explained:

I feel like there's times when even as a White man, I would say that would be more extreme if you were a Black guy, but that women are threatened in ways that were unexpected to me and often the way that I make them more comfortable is by showing the **queer**ness.

Finally, as Taye noted, Black males are perceived by non-Blacks as threats. This illustrates the ways that racism and how one is racially positioned in the United States can significantly restrict one's ability to safely move through the world without constant challenges to one's identity. Black trans* people report higher rates of violence, criminalization, and scrutiny by law enforcement than their White counterparts, although they are surpassed by Native Americans in negative interactions with police (James et al. 2016). The capital of Whiteness is far reaching and cumulative in its effects on life domains such as education, work, and healthcare (see for example Smedley 2012).

These examples represent some of the ways in which embodied capital enables individuals to avoid or manage the specific challenges they encounter in daily life. I turn now to an analysis of the hierarchies that circulate in many trans* spaces and dialogues. The ways in which forms of embodied capital are tied to class capital are more directly discussed in the following chapter. These "Hierarchies of Stigma" to be examined significantly draw on embodied capital in concert with racism, racial hierarchies, and economic inequality in the United States.

DISCUSSION QUESTIONS

1. Define the concept of capital as it relates to sex and gender. In discussing embodied capital, what is the difference between gender congruence capital and sex category capital?
2. Which of these two forms of embodied capital do you believe is more difficult to obtain? Is embodied capital static once achieved? Explain.

3. In what ways do these forms of embodied capital intersect with other statuses a person may hold such as social class, sex category, age, or race?

Notes

1. "Passing" is a problematic term, born in the U.S. of a racist history, used to refer to a person able to be viewed by others as white without having all-white ancestry. I note here the difficult history and use of the term in reference to trans* people. However, its common usage in trans* discourse makes it useful here for legibility. "Passing" as a goal for trans* people is also critiqued within some trans* discourse, for example in Roen 2002.
2. Schilt (2010) categorizes all of her informants as "trans men." I questioned the accuracy of this categorization and the problem it presents for sex and gender as distinct concepts under "separating sex and gender" in Chapter One.
3. The Saturday Night Live archives are available at http://snl.jt.org/index.html and Pat can be searched under Characters.
4. At times, this confusion leads to observers using gender (i.e. dress and hairstyle) to determine sex, assuming that the person is correctly performing gender. In this sense, weight can increase a person's gender congruence capital since gender is being used to determine sex and therefore the two are viewed as congruent by default.
5. For example see Fausto-Sterling 2000.
6. Field notes December 20, 2013.
7. Although commonly referred to as one's gender marker, the designation on legal documentation is male or female, which are designations of sex/sex category, not gender.
8. See note 8.
9. Due to several cues in the exchange and popular discourse, I am fairly convinced the confused representative thought I was clarifying my status because I identified as a trans* female, was clearly *not* doing gender very well, and must be very early in my transition. A source of some amusement for myself and friends for days to come.

3 Hierarchies of Stigma

One thing about me is that I did things the right way. When I decided to do my transition, I took it slow. I didn't go fast. I just took it slow. I was serious about it. When I was coming up . . . as a trans* girl, I'm from the old school. We made it a vow to blend in society without being known as a trans* girl or a, I'm trying to think of something we used back then, a t-girl. A t-girl back then, we blended in. We went to straight clubs and we did everything with straight people. It was different. Now everybody wants to be known as trans*. I'm a trans* this, I'm a trans* that. I'm sick of it . . . The difference I see here, in [a southeastern metropolis], I'm going to speak of, I think the girls play in drag versus being serious. There's probably in the group that we go to, probably two successful serious White transgender girls that live their life as a woman and look the part. The rest of them, I think, it's like playing to me.

—Monique

In his 1963 monograph *Stigma: Notes on the Management of Spoiled Identity*, Erving Goffman discussed attributes that could be used to discredit an individual or group, casting them as outsiders to societal expectations. Stigmatized attributes are used to create "out-groups," or those who are excluded from certain activities or social relationships. Since the publishing of Goffman's ([1963] 1986) work on the subject, scholars have expanded on the topic of stigmatized, or spoiled, identities. The elaboration most relevant to discussion here was an exploration of the ways in which groups are stigmatized by society for failing to meet social expectations and the ways in which hierarchies of stigma are held within the stigmatized group. For example, in the 2011 film *Dark Girls*, Berry and Duke examined the colorism that exists within Black communities and its effects on those with darker skin (see also Herring, Keith, and Horton 2004; Hochschild and Weaver 2007; Hunter 2007). In this example, racism sets Black Americans aside as a stigmatized group overall. Within this stigmatized group, another set of expectations gives those with lighter skin a higher status and those with the darkest pigmentation the most stigmatized position.

As the opening quote from Monique suggests, there are divisions within the stigmatized group of trans* people. In this chapter, I examine two versions of what I call "trans*-er than thou" hierarchies that emerged in my interviews with trans* individuals living in various regions of the United States. These operated in combination with hierarchies created by racism and classism within trans* communities. First, I explore what Katrina Roen (2002) called the "liberal transsexual politics" hierarchy, in which more surgeries and an increased ability to pass is equated with being "more trans*." Second, I examine the "radical politics of gender transgression" (Roen 2002: 502) version of the hierarchy, where being more visibly trans* or genderqueer is viewed as more progressive, and therefore, "more trans*." Like Roen, I found evidence of these same hierarchical divisions in my research and draw the name "trans*-er than thou" from a workshop by the same name, offered at the 2011 Gender Odyssey conference in Seattle, Washington.[1] Next, I explore issues of personal authenticity, class, and geographical considerations I then examine the racial hierarchy in relation to trans* community

Finally, I examine the difficulties associated with stigma hierarchies and what a hierarchy operating inside the already stigmatized group does to those already stigmatized by society.

"More Trans*" as More Passable and More Medical Modifications

Monique, from the introductory quote, was in her late forties and identified as a Black trans* female. Very much viewed as unquestionably female, people were likely surprised to find out she was trans*. For Monique, and many other trans* females, this was the point. Although she lived in the bustling urban area of Ft. Lauderdale, Florida when we met, she grew up in the rural south as one of few Black people in her hometown. Monique's beliefs about seriousness, meaning trans* people should blend in, are hardly uncommon, and are also based in early medical support for trans* people.

In the early days of transition and gender clinics in the 1960s United States, the medical and psychiatric professions provided plenty of reinforcement, intentional or not, for a hierarchy where those who had undergone more medical treatment and were more "passable" were "more trans*." Harry Benjamin, a prominent endocrinologist who researched, advocated for, and treated transsexuals, created a "Sex Orientation Scale" for the purpose of diagnosis and treatment (Meyerowitz 2002). Those listed as "high intensity transsexuals" were most likely to be referred for treatment. In this sense, those whom Benjamin considered higher on the spectrum toward transsexuality would be those permitted to gain access to treatment. As a result, those he and other doctors deemed "more trans*" were allowed to *become* "more trans*." Stryker (2008) argued that when medical transition became available in the United States, doctors used it to re-stabilize the connection between sex and gender. She explained that an androgynous chic took hold in the 1960s as a direct commentary against militaristic masculinity associated with the Vietnam War. In order to reconnect masculinity with male bodies and femininity with female bodies, only those who would present as female and feminine or male and masculine were provided access to medical treatment. Those who would present as female and androgynous or male and androgynous were not provided access (Stryker 2008).

Doctors, therefore, attempted to distinguish sex, gender, and sexuality "deviants" from one another, in part to determine whom to treat with hormones and surgery. These same people were simultaneously trying to distinguish themselves from each other. According to Joanne Meyerowitz (2002), one purpose of these distinctions for trans* people was to avoid stigma by placing it onto others. Meyerowitz explained:

> While the doctors wrestled with definitions and diagnoses, self-identified homosexuals, transvestites, and transsexuals engaged in a parallel practice in which they tried to distinguish themselves from one another. They hoped to make themselves intelligible to others and also to convince doctors, courts, and the public to accord them dignity, rights, and respect. Some chose to align themselves with other sexual and gender variants or wondered out loud which of the existing categories best embraced their sense of themselves. But mostly, it seems, they hoped to explain their differences . . . Those who identified as homosexual, transvestite, or transsexual sometimes attempted to lift their own group's social standing by foisting the stigma of transgression onto others.
>
> (2002: 176–177)

Stryker (2008) agreed with Meyerowitz (2002) that many trans* people hoped to explain their differences and that explanations were riddled with judgments about which people should carry the burden of stigma. Stryker pointed out:

Variants of the word [transgender] had been popping up in male cross-dresser and transvestite communities since the late 1960s, when words such as "transgenderal," "transgenderist," and "transgenderism" were used by people such as Ari Kane and Virginia Prince to describe individuals, such as themselves, who occupied a different gender category from either transvestites or transsexuals.

(2008: 123)[2]

This process of gaining social standing through claims about transgression was demonstrated in Roen's (2002) narratives and in discussions with participants in this and a previous study of mine (Seeber 2013). From the "more trans*," meaning more "passable" perspective, as Monique stated above, "We made it a vow to blend in society without being known as a trans* girl." By making a concerted effort to blend in, Monique and others who talk about blending in as their goal, pointed out that one implicit goal was to be viewed as less transgressive and therefore less warranting of stigmatization. In part, a desire to be viewed as less transgressive and to be less stigmatized comes from the associated risks. Anne, a White 56-year-old trans* female working in an **LGBTQ** organization on the west coast stated that "being my generation, it really was all about the binary. You either fit here or there for lots of reason. Safety is one of them."

In the course of conducting interviews, I heard talk about being serious, others not being serious, and about being taken seriously from Nima (introduced in Chapter One) in addition to Monique. It appeared that "seriousness" was something of a shorthand code about blending in or "passing" as female, and that not being serious was a negative evaluation of a person's behavior and identity. For example, Nima said that once her breasts started to grow from hormones, she left a more androgynous space in her own identity and in the perception of others, but still felt she was not "womanly enough." She recalled a sense of social pressure from other trans* females coming from comments such as, "Girl, when are you going to take it further? Are you really taking this serious?" Unfortunately, in attempting to create a more female appearance and be more "serious," Nima sought out "pumping" services, which nearly killed her and left her face permanently disfigured—as detailed in the telling of her story in Chapter One. Of course, one glaring obstacle in the "more trans*" equals more passable and more medical modifications equation is that the modifications, including those that contribute to passability, are far from free—a point I return to later in this chapter.

"More Trans*" as More "Progressive," More Visually Ambiguous, or Incongruent

In the 1990s, a significant shift occurred in academic discussion about sex and gender identities. This occurred within a broader intellectual move toward poststructuralist/queer theory, which took familiar notions and categories of identity and "deconstructed" them. The social construction of gender and the casting aside of theorizing about bodies crafted a new trajectory within academic debates, which can be seen from the proliferation of articles and texts that examined gender phenomena from the West and Zimmerman (1987) perspective of "Doing Gender" and the Butlerian (1988, 1990, 1993) "performativity" approach. These two perspectives on gender privileged discussions about gender while deemphasizing bodies. In fact, bodies tended to disappear altogether or get reframed as issues of gender as explained in Chapter One. In one such example that specifically related to trans* identity and transition, Judith Shapiro wrote of the "Persistence of Gender and the Mutability of Sex" in which she claimed:

> In its suspension of the usual anatomical recruitment rule to gender category membership, transsexualism raises

questions about what it means to consider sex as the "basis" for systems of gender difference. At the same time, the ability of traditional gender systems to absorb, or even require, such forms of gender-crossing[3] as transsexualism leads us to a more sophisticated appreciation of the power of gender as a principle of social and cultural order. While transsexualism reveals that a society's gender system is a trick done with mirrors, those mirrors are the walls of our species' very real and only home.

(1991: 248–249)

It was clear from Shapiro's (1991) argument about the "maintenance of a society's gender system through the detachment of gender from the very principle that provides its apparent foundation," (272) and a discussion of gender conservatism among transsexuals that Shapiro saw all of us as trapped within a system of gender (roles, behaviors). But none were more trapped (or misguided) than the transsexuals who changed their bodies, thereby maintaining the gender system even without the "usual anatomical recruitment rule to gender category" (1991: 248). Roen also noted that around the time of Shapiro's (1991) work, "recent academic and political articulations of transgenderism privilege **crossing** over passing" (2002: 504). Roen explained that the preferred "crossing" meant living as visually sex and gender incongruent (female and masculine, male and feminine) or as openly transsexual, rather than attempting to blend in with cis* males and females. Trans* scholar Namaste agreed with Roen's assessment, critiquing work by Judith "Jack" Halberstam (1998) in which, "Halberstam contends that **FTM** transgendered people need to be queer" (2000: 64). Halberstam's directive that trans* males be queer similarly meant living as visually incongruent or openly trans*.

The focus of my research has been with people who have made modifications to their bodies, regardless of binary or non-binary sex and/or gender identification. For this reason, the majority of evidence I have for this second "more trans*"—meaning more non-conforming and more progressive—narrative came from participant discussions about how this "progressive" narrative and their understandings of the social construction of gender inhibited their decision-making processes toward bodily modifications. In a previous study Yav, a 54-year-old, White, petite, masculine-identified, retired, disabled veteran, talked about the difficulties reconciling his particular feminist perspective with his desire to change his body:

> So one thing that was difficult for me because I lived in San Francisco from the mid-early 70s to, 'til I went in the air force in 1979, and during that time it was just real big, you know, the heavy separatist lesbian feminists and of course the straight women with the ERA[4] and everything was men were bad . . . Butch women were hated because we were identifying as men and men were the enemy.
>
> (Seeber 2013: 36)

Yav had been on testosterone hormone therapy for 6 months when we spoke and had future plans for chest reconstruction surgery. However, as he pointed out, it took much longer to get to the point of making bodily modifications because the idea of changing his body was contradictory to the notions of lesbian separatist feminism in which he was raised.

Loki, a 34-year-old, White, trans* male had spent 8 years on testosterone while working as a social worker on the west coast. He was sporting a beard when we sat down for an interview and spoke about a similarly personal/political relationship to socially constructed gender and body modification. Being 20 years Yav's junior, Loki formed his relationship to social construction differently, but had a similar difficulty reconciling his personal and political beliefs with desires for bodily modification. He commented:

I wanna be genderqueer for a while because I wanna break this binary system and then you're like yipes! I need so desperately to be read as something that I don't care if it's super masculine . . . I feel like there was that time period where genderqueer was really okay because I was like yeah, I don't need to fit into some box. And then when you're in that really awkward stage where you really don't fit into any boxes . . . I felt so foundationless, that I really needed some sort of stability, and that box was that stability.

(Seeber 2013: 37)

While some feel comfortable and stable without a box to fit into, for Loki, this position clearly created difficulties with his sense of an authentic self.

It is understandable from the "progressive" narrative of non-conformity that there exists an underlying assumption that because gender, or more accurately the link between sexed bodies and gender behaviors, is socially constructed, those who change their bodies do so in the interests of "**matching**." For example, someone assigned male at birth would pursue making the body female to match the desire to perform femininity. This changing of the body in order to "match" then paints those who medically modify their bodies as dupes of the gender system. Non-conforming people are then, by contrast, less warranting of stigma from their perspective, just as those who make bodily changes see themselves as less warranting of stigma from the "trans*-er than thou" perspective of more surgeries and more passable means "more trans*."

In her analysis of the two perspectives, which she pointed out, are not mutually exclusive, Roen (2002) noted that this newer "more genderqueer, more progressive equals 'more trans*'" narrative had recently become the more privileged narrative. She also explained that from this perspective, "those who seek to pass as women or men are described as being 'closeted' or having 'false consciousness'" (521). Roen (2002) also highlighted that being out, or openly trans*, which is expected from this "more progressive" stance, was difficult and sometimes impossible for trans* people who were differently located in society. She further explored how activists expecting trans* people to take up the "more progressive" approach "(1) fail to take into account the diversity of context and experience of transpeople [sic] and (2) do not accurately conceptualize how agentic subjects maneuver among apparently competing discourses" by using parts of the "more passable" and "more progressive" narratives strategically and in combination (Roen 2002: 521). In the following section, I attend to the difficulties with both of these "trans*-er than thou" narratives, drawing on Roen's (2002) critiques in addition to exploring issues of individual authenticity not yet represented in this chapter.

Bodies, Behaviors, and Personal Authenticity

Two significant problems in the hierarchical logic of a "trans*-er than thou" narrative are that difficulties with bodies and behaviors are separate issues, and that personal authenticity has considerable importance. First, the earlier version of "more trans*" by virtue of being more passable and having had more medical modifications focuses on having a problem with the body itself and addressing that issue through medical means. The more recent version of "more trans*" is based on breaking down the socially constructed binary of sex/gender. In this version, the problem resides in society's insistence that only female bodies can behave in a feminine fashion and male bodies only in a masculine fashion. Society insists there can be no mixing of masculinity and femininity and no "crossing" sex category with gender, meaning no putting together of female bodies and masculinity or male bodies and femininity.

If an individual has a problem with the body, using medicine and medical technologies for the modification of the body itself is a reasonable solution. If instead an individual has an issue of "matching" a binary sex and sex category to a binary gender (behaviors), this is a problem regarding the social construction of gender. For this reason, the solution is logically a social one based on dismantling the faulty logic that assumes femininity springs forth from female biology and masculinity from male biology. It replaces that logic with the understanding that the "matching" of sex and sex category to gender is a *social* requisite and largely a process of socialization (Seeber 2013). The considerably different nature of the two problems—one of body/medicine and the other of "matching" sex category with gender/social construction—makes comparing solutions a futile enterprise.

Related to attempts to make a comparison between—and hierarchy from—two different and dissimilar problems is the second difficulty regarding the idea of a progressive narrative itself. If authenticity is the ultimate goal for trans* people, how is it progressive for someone with an issue of the body to maintain the sex assigned to them at birth and instead live as gender non-conforming? As I mentioned with Yav and Loki, participants in my previous study spoke of the impediment this progressive narrative of gender non-conformity posed to realizing their authentic selves. For an example specifically about authenticity, Taylor was 39-years-old and a year and a half into medical modifications when I met him. He was a White non-profit director on the west coast and he described both his sex and gender as mixed and "not that simple," but also applied "transgender man" as an identity for himself. Taylor was well educated in the concept of the social construction of gender and about the activism aimed at breaking down binary assumptions and expectations of gender. He shared how the notion of a "more progressive" understanding of gender created a barrier to realizing his authentic sense of embodiment:

All the activist in me was like why? Why would I, why do I need to change my body in order to have an identity I wanna have? And fuck the world, and I can be however I wanna be and . . . so I struggled with that activist identity of I can be genderqueer, I don't believe in two genders anyway and all of that. And so I'm one of those people that's like ok, I'm a believer now, I don't know why this is how far I needed to go exactly, but I feel amazing, now.

(Seeber 2013: 37)

It does not seem progressive for someone with a body issue, with or without a gender "matching" issue, to live as gender non-conforming and in the sex category they were assigned at birth. The idea of authenticity also begs the question: in what way would it be progressive for someone with an issue regarding society's requirement of sex and gender "matching" to change their body if they have no problem with their body the way it is? There is the additional possibility that someone has both a problem with their body and a problem with the social requirement to "match." In that case, medical modification of the body in conjunction with post-modification non-matching would be the best, most "progressive" goal for that individual. For example, someone may be assigned male at birth and feel that their body should be female, but prefer a masculine female identity and presentation. Having a sense of oneself as female does not require a sense of oneself as feminine. Progressive then makes little sense in a discussion about two different problems with very different solutions (Seeber 2013).

Considering Class and Geographic Location

A further challenge to any "trans*-er than thou" narrative has to do with the differing abilities of people to achieve or live authentically based on economic capital or situational location

In a narrative where "more trans*" means more medical modifications, economic capital is a significant limitation to access. By comparison to surgical procedures, hormones are relatively cheap and may even be free in areas able to provide free treatment for the economically disadvantaged. As of now, surgeries for trans* people to create their authentic selves are rarely covered by health insurance. Even if some health insurance policies do cover these surgeries, we must still ask who is able to pay the co-payment and patient percentage of the bill as well as how common it is for specific sectors of the trans* community to have access to these particular health insurance plans in the first place.

The cost of medical modification means a class component is involved in the ability for people to achieve a sense of authentic self, but also means that class is involved for many in the ability to purchase embodied capital of sex category. Medical procedures such as hormones or facial feminization surgeries make it much easier for trans* people to be viewed by others as either male or female rather than somewhere in between. Trans* people for whom a binary sex category either feels authentic or is acceptable—meaning I may not identify as male, but I accept others

Table 3.1 Estimated Costs for Selected Surgical Procedures and Hormone Replacement Therapy for Trans* Females

Male-to-Female (MTF) Surgery and Hormone Replacement Therapy	Cost Estimate
Breast augmentation	$5,000–$8,200
Orchiectomy	$2,500–$4,600
Vaginoplasty with labiaplasty[a]	$14,500–$29,300
Hormones	$20–$200/mo

Source: costhelper.com; Dr. Toby Meltzer; srsmiami.com; thetransgendercenter.com; :sroadmap.com.

Notes: surgical cost estimate includes surgeon, hospital, and anesthesia fees without insurance. Does not include consultation fees, bloodwork, therapy required for hormone/surgery letters from therapist, surgery medications, travel costs, or lodging and food if required to stay nearby for follow-up care.

highest estimate includes **vaginoplasty**, **labiaplasty**, and **orchiectomy**.

Table 3.2 Estimated Costs for Selected Surgical Procedures and Hormone Replacement Therapy for Trans* Males

Female-to-Male (FTM) Surgery and Hormone Replacement Therapy	Cost Estimate
Chest reconstruction	$3,500–$8,100
Hysterectomy with oophorectomy	$10,000–$20,000
Metoidioplasty[a]	$10,700–$64,525
Phalloplasty[b]	$21,250–$150,000
Hormones	$25–$200/mo

Source: costhelper.com; Dr. Jens Berli; Dr. Toby Meltzer; ftmguide.org; srsmiami.com; Strohecker's pharmacy; thetransgendercenter.com.

Notes: surgical cost estimate includes surgeon, hospital, and anesthesia fees without insurance. Does not include consultation fees, bloodwork, therapy required for hormone/surgery letters from therapist, surgery medications, travel costs, or lodging and food if required to stay nearby for follow-up care.

[a] lowest estimate includes **metoidioplasty**, scrotoplasty, testicular implants, and glansplasty. Highest estimate also includes **vaginectomy**, hysterectomy with **oophorectomy**, and **urethroplasty**.

[b] lowest estimate includes **phalloplasty**, scrotoplasty, testicular implants, glansplasty, and transposition of the clitoris. Highest estimate also includes vaginectomy, hysterectomy with oophorectomy, and urethroplasty.

categorizing me as male generally—who also have high levels of class capital can, in essence, buy their way out of the ongoing challenges of being difficult for others to sex categorize.

Class status also relates to challenges associated with gender congruence capital. In the "more trans*" as more passable narrative, higher status is achievable through higher levels of class capital. Interestingly, higher class status also works to provide higher status through the alternative "more trans*" as more non-conforming narrative as well. The rules surrounding gender behavior are far more stringent at the bottom. In working-class or blue-collar spaces, males are rigidly expected to be masculine. And while more flexibility may exist for females regarding performances of masculinity and femininity, females who are more masculine risk being stigmatized as lesbians because of their gender performance, which is then its own loss of social capital. By contrast, the greater autonomy and lower surveillance of many white-collar positions comes with increased flexibility for gender non-conformity. So while someone visually gender non-binary may accrue less gender congruence capital, not having that capital at the top of the class hierarchy is less problematic. The increase in flexibility for non-conformity is not equally experienced by all, however. Non-conformity brings with it the risk of exclusion or discrimination, and while that risk is less pronounced higher up the class ladder, other forms of inequality complicate this picture. For example, it is riskier for someone who also faces racial discrimination to perform their authentic sense of gender non-conformity, even in higher positions of class status.

From the perspective of "more trans*" as more medical modification, the out-of-pocket expenses for surgical procedures are also dependent on geographic location. There are only a few surgical specialists throughout the United States who provide transition surgeries. Depending on where a person lives, they may have to travel a significant distance to where a surgeon is located. Surgery also requires healing and follow-up care, which increases travel, lodging, food, and the costs of other necessities. Travel may also require deciding between a more difficult experience due to going alone or the added expense of bringing someone along to provide necessary care-giving, as many surgeries result in limitations to mobility or other limitations to self-care. And because economic status is closely tied to ethno-racial status in the United States, a hierarchy based on economic capital is also a hierarchy based on ethno-racial status.

Geographic location also plays an important role from the perspective of "more trans*" meaning more non-conforming. Some geographical locations such as large urban areas may provide more acceptance in the sense of fewer negative social sanctions for sex and gender non-conforming people than suburban areas due to the increased diversity of identities in urban spaces. In addition to issues of social sanctions, urban areas may also provide a broader set of representations of what sex and gender identities are possible, making it easier to envision and then live a more non-conforming life. For example, in a previous research study I met Jay, a 40-year-old, White "masculinely leaning androgynous female." At the time, she was six years post chest reconstruction surgery. Jay explained to me how geographic location made a difference in deciding on how she wanted her body configured. She explained:

> I just knew that I wanted that [chest reconstruction] physical modification and at that point it's like I said, I fluctuate. Like I'm a female, but I'm also boyish and masculine and I've been fortunate enough being here in this [urban center] tiny little microcosm of the states, to have people totally accept the way I look and not have a problem with it and just be like "whatever," you know? And I think I said before, it made me feel less pressure to choose a side, because maybe if I stayed there [suburban town], maybe I would have become an FTM.
>
> (Seeber 2013: 55)

Do We See White Privilege? In Polite Company? In Mixed Company?

In addition to discussing the impact of class and geographic location on how one is situated within internal hierarchies of trans* communities, I examine here the racial hierarchies that are also in place. Trans* communities are no less fraught with racial biases than the general population of the United States. While often unconscious, or **implicit biases**,[5] these biases are made obvious through the responses I received to asking about how race impacted participants' stories. When asked about the ways she felt race may have made a difference in the challenge she did or did not face, Leddy replied:

I would be the first to admit that if you're not White you're at a disadvantage, full stop. The only reason I got the job I've got was because I interviewed as a White male. But for that fact I wouldn't be where I am. I'd say race is a huge part [of the challenges I do/do not face as trans*], especially the industries in particular that I work is very White. I hate to say it's a bigoted field, but it is. It's very bigoted so there's no way to sugarcoat that.

Not everyone I interviewed was as clear about the role of racism in the intersecting exclusions trans* people face as the quote from Leddy may suggest. Feminist scholars in critical Whiteness studies have examined the contours of Whiteness for decades—what it is, how it operates, how its privileges are hidden from people qualified for Whiteness, and how discussion of its privileges are ignored (Frankenberg 1993; McIntosh 1998; Pratt 1984; Segrest 1994; Twine 1996). Having benefitted from this long history of feminist scholars, Karyn McKinney (2005) vividly pointed out in *Being White: Stories of Race and Racism*, that White people, myself included, were raised to not see—or to assert color-blindness as a form of White innocence—the privileges of Whiteness within the United States. Without conscious education and effort, these privileges remain invisible to many White Americans, contributing to the unconscious or implicit nature of biases around race. Challenges associated with race are recast as some other issue, the advantageous position is reimagined as the disadvantaged using a single example from a much larger individual narrative (rather than a structural or group level analysis), or deflected altogether, perhaps as something not discussed in polite conversation or that has not been given much thought.

In one example of recasting race/ethnicity issues as something else, Eduardo, a Latino, 36-year-old trans* male, talked about the gossip of Latinx culture rather than talking about race and ethnicity per se. First, he pointed out that where he grew up was ethnically Latinx, ruling out significant issues of minority status. Eduardo then switched to talking about culture and commented, "we tend to gossip a lot too. It just goes with the territory being Latino . . . so in a small town like this people know your business and people know what you are about and they know who you are." Indeed, the town is 81 percent Latinx according to Census 2010, so in day-to-day life being perceived as a man of color may have had little impact on his embodied capital so long as Eduardo remained within the small town or the racially/ethnically diverse surrounding Bay Area.

Two White individuals, one genderqueer person and one trans* female, provided examples of Whiteness being viewed as a disadvantageous position. In particular, these stories echoed the stories about race studied by McKinney (2005), and it is important to keep in mind that these stories about Whiteness as a disadvantage are "fictions," as McKinney noted. As she pointed out, "these fictions are part of the collective experience of Whiteness—none of these individuals needs to be maliciously racist for these fictions to survive and sustain racism" (xviii). I examined these stories as did McKinney as "stories and discourses representing whiteness" and I agree with her statement that "whites can help other whites to see that elite whites, not people of color, are responsible for the economic pressures on middle-class and working-class whites" (2005: xviii–xix).

In the first example, Alex, a 39-year-old, White individual who identified as "somewhere between genderqueer, trans*, F to M, dyke," spoke of being pushed out of an organizing role for a group that was not designed as a space specifically for people of color.[6] She[7] was repeatedly told that people of color should occupy leadership roles. Alex found the requests for him to step down particularly confusing seeing as people sometimes perceived Alex as non-White on the basis of her small stature. Moreover, those asking that she step down so that people of color could fill leadership positions were likely *not* viewed by others as people of color and/or were unwilling to actually fill the leadership roles. When asked about the effects of race, this was the only example Alex mentioned.

In a similar fashion to Alex, Zoe (previously discussed in Chapter Two regarding sex category capital) described learning she was HIV positive prior to transition and how she proceeded to research extensively about the resources available to help manage her chronic condition and sustain herself. Zoe, having earned only a GED, was working in unskilled labor positions outdoors and, when diagnosed with HIV, was told by her doctor that she had no blood platelets. She was informed that she might have to go on disability because, "They said if I got cut I would bleed to death, you know." During her research, Zoe was disappointed to discover that:

> Everything that I found was that if you were female, if you were African-American, or something else, but if you were a White male, there was nothing . . . you know, listed as a White male . . . So it got frustrating because everything seemed to me like it was designed for African-American people or females that are having a hard time . . . Well, what it boiled down to, I had a house and two cars in the driveway. I could not get disability because of that. I had to be living out on the street as a White male in order to get disability . . . I was going to lose everything, you know, because of no help.

One thing absent from Zoe's analysis of not finding help is precisely McKinney's (2005) point above about *White elites* creating the difficulty. The problem lies in how the rules for who receives assistance are written and elite Whites control the rules of the disability system. A second missing piece of this analysis is that receiving the benefits of White privilege, simply by being socially perceived as White, is a resource that likely played a significant part in someone with a GED education being able to earn enough to save up for a house and two cars in the first place. So while the loss is understandably regrettable and frustrating at an individual level, from the perspective of how racialized groups fare in the United States, Zoe's accumulated wealth before her diagnosis was higher than average for someone with Zoe's level of education and who was dark-skinned Black or Latinx. In her analysis of fictions of Whiteness as a position of disadvantage, McKinney argued that:

> the forcefulness of these statements should be judged in light of the fact that fundamental ideologies of Whiteness deny both the suggestion that Whiteness brings economic privilege, and the policies used to remedy this inequality.
> (2005: 150)

In addition to her belief in the economic disadvantage of being listed as a White male, Zoe commented on the cultural disadvantage of Whiteness—another area covered by McKinney's (2005) analysis. Zoe shared:

> Then it kind of bothered me, too, because I do know that [African-Americans] have their own pride. Well, if you are a White person and you have something that is White only, that ain't going to float, but African-Americans can do that and nothing is said. So that kind of rubs me raw, but don't get me wrong, I am not a prejudiced person, never was and never will be, you know. That is not my issue. My issue is that it got to the point where I do feel like that it is really harmful in some ways because there is just no help for some people that need it and it is not coming to them because they are White and they are male—especially when it comes to something as serious as HIV. I mean some things, sure I can let slide, so if they want to have their own African-American cruise, they want to have their own pride, I have no problem with that. I mean that is fine, but you know, if I say well,

I want to throw this big cruise but it is White only, some will get pissed off at me. But I would never do that. I mean that is not my style.

This is precisely the kind of "whiteness as culturally stigmatized" story McKinney (2005) unpacked. She pointed out that Whites talk about people of color as being oversensitive. Part of this, she stated, was that, "for many respondents, the chaos of racism is in the past, and it is now *Whites* with a burden that people of color do not have: they must be careful not to 'offend' people who still think about the past" (2005: 116; emphasis in original). The very violent and discriminatory *power* realities, both historically and currently, of White only spaces are what make them offensive, not the perceptions of those who do not qualify as White. Still, the stereotypes about oversensitivity pointed to implicit biases held by those who made claims about people of color being oversensitive.

For some Whites, the fictions of Whiteness as a position of disadvantage can and do coexist alongside ideas about the disadvantages of not being qualified for Whiteness. After discussing her views about how Whiteness had negatively impacted her life, Zoe also pointed out that when it comes to hate crimes, it is more likely for African-Americans to suffer. She said, "It tends to be when you hear of a murder in the trans* community, it was an African-American person or something like that."

In contrast to the disadvantage beliefs discussed, most White participants said very little, acknowledged that it might have been an issue for others, or deflected the conversation by saying it was "not my experience." For example, when asked how race has affected the challenges she has or has not faced and the resources she has had for managing them, 52-year-old, White trans* female Heather's first response was, "Now what do you mean my race?" I followed up by asking, "So, in terms of being White in a dominant White society, do you think that that has made a difference in terms of the challenges that you faced or that you haven't had to that you have seen other folks who maybe identify as a different race and had to face or whatnot in sort of a journey . . ." at which point she cut in and declared, "I can't think about how somebody else will be because I don't know what it is like to be Black." While strictly speaking this is true, Heather went on to recognize that there was a fight others had that she did not, meaning racism. However, she then talked about how she worked to blend in to society, to not stick out, and the drive she had for that, and ended with, "I don't know if anybody has that drive like I had." Rather than talk about White privilege or systemic racism, the discussion veered off into one about motivation for blending in and the personal drive to do so.

There is a chance that saying something was "not my experience" may be based in the way trans* identity is often discussed from a personal standpoint rather than being said as a deflection. Particularly in activist circles or in media outlets, trans* people often make sure to clearly point out that they are only able to speak from their own experience. This is done to acknowledge that there are as many ways of being trans* as there are trans* people and that trans* identity is inherently about self-determination—that is, the only person who can decide if I am truly trans* or not is me. And, to be fair, it is also possible that the wording of my question contributed to some of the short responses I received. The question asked, "In what ways do you feel *race* has affected the challenges you have or have not faced and the resources you have for managing them?" While my question sought to determine the challenges a person did or did not have, framing the question as being about challenges may have led some people to only think about negative experiences with race. This may have also contributed to people only thinking about those who have had negative experience with race, not Whites, having anything to say about race at all. Out of thirty interviews, however, more than half pointed out the existence of White privilege, and other Whites viewed

Whiteness as a disadvantage, making it more likely that "not my experience" and one-sentence answers were signaling a blindness to race issues that Whites have been socialized to have since birth, or possibly a deflection of the conversation.

Whites were not the only ones to deflect conversations about race, although the purpose seems somewhat different among trans* females of color who did this. For example, Monique, 49 years old and Black, dressed in a lightweight black and white sleeveless dress at the time of our meeting, with her long hair straightened and pulled back in a ponytail, and not visibly trans* declared:

> I don't even talk about race much because I haven't had any race issues that much. I grew up in a little small town and it was a White town. I had to learn to live with White folks. I've really not had a real bad struggle. Of course, I've probably been called a nigger. In the little town I grew up in White people were here and whatever the case may be, that wasn't a struggle for me. That's just how life was.

According to Census 2000, the rural zip code where Monique grew up was 86.1 percent White with a population under 8,000. By Census 2010, the racial demographics had changed little and the White population was at 85.4 percent. Here, the deflection served the purpose of minimizing the difficulties associated with the racism of Whites, not revealing blindness to White privilege or a discomfort in discussing it. The reason for minimizing the difficulties became clearer as Maya similarly noted, "I wouldn't say it's been a challenge for me. I haven't experienced much racism, but I do feel like in society transgender women of color have it harder than White trans* women." Maya then talked about being African-American, a trans* female, and that:

> I also didn't want that to be a crutch or I don't ever want to use that as an excuse because anything could be turned

around and I've proven that, I feel, I worked very hard for
what I have today. I endured a lot but it was worth it.

This illustrated McKinney's (2005) point about accusations that
people of color are oversensitive about the past.

Minimizing the difficulties faced, or not using difficulties
posed by racism "as an excuse," appeared to be ways of avoiding
being accused of oversensitivity. This approach also focused on
owning the hard work put in rather than having accomplish-
ments cast aside as a matter of having targeted programs directed
at you (as in Zoe's beliefs about the availability of funding for
minorities). The minimization of difficulties relayed to others
"I worked for this, it was not handed to me, and I am not here
crying asking for someone to hand things to me." It was a
response very cognizant of ongoing racism and an attempt to
disrupt it. In part, this tactic of minimization may have been
directly related to Monique and Maya's perceptions of me as a
White male—Lisa, also a Black trans* female, first brought up
her nervousness about talking about her life and experiences with
me when I asked about the effects of race near the end of our
interview. However, it also seemed likely that this was an ongoing
tactic of surviving and thriving in a racist society.

"More Trans*" as a Zero-Sum Game

One final problem evident in the discourse about who is "more
trans*" and less deserving of stigma is the reality that this is a
zero-sum game: for someone to be more accepted and less
stigmatized, someone else has to be less accepted and more stigmatized. Regardless of which version of "more trans*" hold
sway, as with classism and racial biases within trans* communities, efforts are being targeted inward so that trans* people of
varying identities expend energy toward making judgments and
not simply acknowledging differences. In doing so, trans* peopl

divide-and-conquer among themselves in a fashion that speaks to Foucault's (1995) notions about surveillance. In particular this speaks to the lower requirements for the dominant or more powerful group to do surveillance when those under scrutiny have learned to observe and report on themselves and those similar to them. In this way, the stigmatization and subjugation of all people who might be considered under the broader identity of trans* can be easily perpetuated with little effort on the part of people uninterested in according respect, dignity, and equality to trans* people. As long as significant oppression continues to exist within the stigmatized group those in power need not work very hard to remain in power.

Making distinctions between varieties of trans* identities is not an inherently damaging practice and can actually promote positive alliances. For example, being conscious of how racial, ethnic, and economic differences situate trans* people with respect to violence, lack of resources, and empathy can help guide movements to consider a wide variety of trans* people and promote attending to the needs of the most vulnerable among us. As I discussed in Chapter Two, some trans* people have more or less gender congruence capital and some have more or less sex category capital. The challenges and needs that arise from each of these types of capital require different strategies to remedy. What becomes damaging in the discussion about "more trans*" is the hierarchical positioning of identities, which rather than promoting alliance building, creates roadblocks to collaboration and social solidarity that are necessary for movements of social change (Snow and Soule 2010). Roen (2002) pointed out that in an atmosphere where some trans* people value passing and others devalue it, exclusions are created "affecting the ability of transpeople [sic] to support one another in their local communities" (504).

Clearly, for a host of reasons, hierarchies of stigma within trans* communities and the logics that maintain them are harmful to the advancement of trans* activism and leading authentic, respected lives. I suggest here and elsewhere (Seeber 2013) that recognizing two conceptually distinct, though potentially overlapping, problems related to sex, sex category, and gender could provide trans* activists a way to dismantle barriers created through the construction of hierarchies between those who have a problem with the body and those who have a problem with the way society declares that only certain bodies can behave in a particular gender fashion. Challenges in racial and class biases would also need to be consciously addressed to remove hierarchies, both with regard to how race and class hierarchies operate alongside "trans*-er than thou" hierarchies and how race, and especially class, are intimately tied to these particular narratives.

It is understandable that every human being wishes to have others see them as they see themselves and to be socially included. Creating stigma hierarchies may be interpreted as a form of self-promotion, enhancing the self-esteem of individuals who have endured injuries to their identities. However, stigma operates in trans* communities, as it does in other communities, as a means of validating and empowering some members' identities at the expense of others. This contributes to ongoing challenges for the community as a whole. In the following chapter I shift to an analysis of three areas of life that are shaped by trans* identity—whether or not trans* identity is claimed openly.

DISCUSSION QUESTIONS

1. Define the two versions of "more trans*" narratives.
2. How are these two narratives related to the distinction the author makes about bodies and behaviors in Chapter One?
3. The author points out that a problem with the body would logically have a medical technology solution, whereas a problem with society's behavior requirements (gender) based on the body would logically have a social solution. How might these two views clash over the inclusion of "gender

dysphoria" in the **Diagnostic and Statistical Manual of Mental Disorders** (DSM) used by clinicians such as psychologists and psychiatrists to diagnose mental disorders? What is gained or lost by each side of the "more trans*" discussion by being included in the DSM?

Notes

1. The workshop description in the conference program reads:

   > It may not be hard for those of us at this conference to reach a consensus regarding the outside world's view of transgender people. We might easily agree that trans people are discriminated against and misunderstood by many in the outside world. But what happens when we ourselves look at the differences within our collective gender communities? Are we just as uninformed and biased in our own thinking as those we consider "outside"? Do we make our own rigid determinations about the "real" ways of being trans? How do we make those determinations? Is it along class lines, for example, financially inaccessible surgeries being considered markers for "real" trans people? Living full time? Appearance? Queerest? This session is not about assigning blame. It's about creating conversations wherein we can each examine our own discomfort with difference. We'll look at these differences with a goal of gaining a fresh perspective and a chance to celebrate our unique lives together.
   >
   > (2011: 49)

2. Stryker points out that Prince is an important part of trans* history and the present trans* political movement, albeit a challenging part given, "her open disdain for homosexuals, her frequently expressed negative opinion of transsexual surgeries, and her conservative stereotypes regarding masculinity and femininity" (2008: 46).

3. To clarify, Shapiro here uses "crossing" to "designate those who are attempting to 'pass' as members of the opposite sex" (1991: 249). Roen

(2002) uses "passing" to refer to this "opposite sex" sense of transsexuality and "crossing" to refer to those who might be identified as genderqueer, or those who, regardless of bodily changes, do not fit within the now-and-always both female and feminine or male and masculine dichotomy.

4. ERA is the acronym for the Equal Rights Amendment.
5. On implicit bias see Greenwald and Banaji 1995; Greenwald, Nosek, and Banaji 2003.
6. I use the term people of color to refer to racial and ethnic minorities who are not perceived by others as able to be categorized as White due to phenotypic characteristics such as skin color, hair texture, etc.
7. Alex uses both masculine and feminine pronouns and prefers having them used interchangeably.

4 Families, Intimacy, and Sexuality

I have family members who have just become much more accepting and understanding because I look **heteronormative** to them. There are areas of my life they don't know about as a result of their overwhelming acceptance of what I look like. For them it's a closed book now. I'm a guy, married to a woman. I'm a psychologist. I'm doing all these great things and they're all happy about that. They kind of leave it there . . . With my godson, every now and then we'll have a conversation where something will come up about my history, or he'll find an old picture of me. He'll say something about it, but if I bring something up he looks at me like confused. He's 19, he knew me when he was little as a female, but he's always seen me as a guy. We go do a lot of guy things together . . . There's no issues, it doesn't really come up at all.

—Michael

Pre-Transition Families: Families We're Raised In and Families We Create

Family relationships can be particularly challenging for trans* people. Of all the relationships we have in our adult lives, the people that make up our **family of origin or orientation** are relationships we do not choose. Certainly, we can decide whether or not to maintain relationships with specific individuals in our family of orientation. However, "blood" or marital relationships of family members are considered important in the social context of the United States. Families we come from can be fraught with differences of all kinds that are difficult to navigate.

Gay and lesbian individuals are often ostracized from their family of orientation as soon as they **come out**, or disclose their identity (Gonsiorek 1988; Savin-Williams 1994; Weston 1991), and many a youth arrive at homelessness through coming out at an early age (Maccio and Ferguson 2016; Reck 2009). In the last decade or two, this narrative of being kicked out of the family home, or placed in circumstances that make leaving home more desirable than staying, appears to be subsiding. Many more gay and lesbian-identified youth are finding tolerance, if not acceptance, in the home rather than being locked in a closet with a bible with parents hoping that would sort them out.[1] The trend of tolerance or acceptance instead of ostracization is, perhaps not surprisingly, delayed among trans*-identified youth. Although Black and Latina trans* females were at the forefront of events that sparked a national LGBTQ movement in the United States, their involvement was often actively erased, contributing to this delay (Stryker 2008). The increased visibility of gay and lesbian people and their social acceptance appears to have changed the realities of how families of orientation deal with having a gay or lesbian identified child. Since the visibility of trans* people and trans* people's mobilization into social movements became more prominent at least two decades later (in the 1990s for trans* compared to 1970s or earlier for gays and lesbians),[2] it should come as no surprise that the ways families handle a trans*-identified child are lagging behind as well.

Like gay and lesbian individuals, trans* people face being rejected by family members when they come out. For youth, coming out most likely means dealing with parents who retain legal control over their lives and siblings. For adults, coming out means dealing with parents and siblings, but because adult trans* individuals are less likely to live with their parents, this is a different experience. However, for adults, coming out may also mean dealing with **conjugal families** or **families of procreation**[3]—a spouse or partner and perhaps one's own children. This typically means dealing with a whole new set of challenges, including legal issues pertaining to marriage, divorce, and child custody depending on how old an individual's children are when they start openly identifying as trans*. For this project, I explicitly looked for people 18 years or older, who had undergone some sort of medical modification to their bodies, and considered themselves 5 or more years into transition. As such, this study deals more with people who came out as adults and faced the challenges of family from that perspective. As people begin to recognize and name themselves trans* at younger and younger ages, more stories will emerge about how families deal with trans* people still under their care and control (see for example Rahilly 2015; Vilmur 2014). For now, I discuss family relationships primarily from the point of view of people who began to identify themselves as trans* during adulthood.

James, a 49-year-old, White trans* male, provided a good example of how one's family of orientation's acceptance of trans* identity lags behind acceptance for lesbian and gay identities. I first met James at a trans* conference, then travelled to the mid-sized city of Lexington, Kentucky where he lived to interview him. I had spent all morning interviewing a couple and had felt a little rushed for time when I arrived. He led me upstairs to

Table 4.1 Experiences of Family Rejection Among Respondents Out to at Least Some of the Immediate Family They Grew Up With

Form of Family Rejection	% of Respondents Out to at Least Some of Immediate Family Grew Up With
Immediate family member stopped communicating or ended relationship	26
Family member was violent	10
Kicked out of the house	8
Not allowed to wear clothes congruent with identity	27
Sent to a professional to change them	14
At least one of these forms of rejection	44

Source: U.S. Transgender Survey (James et al. 2016), N=21,618

his small studio/junior one-bedroom apartment on the top floor of a building that had the slanted ceilings of being in the attic. On the way up the stairs I noticed a high-end road bicycle on the landing a flight below his front door. He had another bicycle hanging from the ceiling in his bedroom. He welcomed me to his "bohemian place" and I noted to myself that it reminded me of apartments in San Francisco—small, quirky, and full of character. James was dressed in blue jeans, a blue crew neck sweatshirt from a university or high school with the name of the school emblazoned on the front, and bright red slippers. His hair was thinning a bit on top—a topic we discussed later and I told him of my own management strategy to keep my hair shaved short in an attempt to bald gracefully. He had thoughtfully purchased a lemon cinnamon roll for each of us and got me a glass of orange juice to go with it as we sat at his small kitchen table to talk.

After reviewing the history of his transition, James looked at the list of possible areas where being trans* had an impact on his life and started at the top of the list with family of origin. He described the losses he had experienced:

I have family that has totally cut me off entirely from their lives. My sister, for about 7 or 8 years, didn't allow me to see her children . . . The really odd thing about all that is that I thought the people that I was closest to that would take it the best or at least try to be supportive were the ones that disappeared on me.

In contrast, there were others in his life he did not believe were particularly close to him who ended up being supportive when he told them about being trans*.

I asked James about how he handled the fallout with family members and he talked about making attempts over the years to reach out and provide people with opportunities to reconnect. He explained that "my sister eventually allowed me to see her kids again a number of years ago, but I don't go home that frequently." James grew up approximately 515 miles from where he was living at the time of interview. On one occasion he tried reaching out to the aunt and uncle he had been close to and prompted, "I'm coming home, maybe I could meet up with you." Shortly after this brief conversation with his aunt, he received a letter from her claiming, "if you really say you love us like you do, don't contact us." Given the geographical distance and the lackluster responses at best from family, James noted, "To me a lot of it's just lost now."

In contrast to James's experience with his family of orientation, Heather shared, "my mom is like my cheerleader." Heather, the 52-year-old, White trans* female from Chapter Three, began transition in the early 1990s, but she noted that, "growing up I just thought I was a little girl." I met Heather at her home, also in Lexington, Kentucky. Because I was unfamiliar with the city and driving a rental car, I was using the GPS on my phone to locate her house. Describing how I located her house I observed, "I was pretty sure I had the right door when saw the lawn filled with ornaments—some for Halloween, but mostly just decorative things you would find in a yard (stereotypically) tended by a woman." Describing her living room I documented:

> The living room was very white, red, pink, and cozy . . . Her place was decorated tastefully in a comfy, feminine way—throw pillows, pastels, white carpet, decorative drapes, lived in but not cluttered—with a touch of tradition and formality—china white/blue vases and decorative plates, dark formal wood looking china cabinet and table with chairs, white table cloth. On a small round glass table between the old-fashioned sitting room armchair I sat in and its mate sat a metalwork candle stand with 7 mosaic style red glass candle cups.[4]

For our interview Heather laid comfortably across the living room from me on a couch wearing a pink hooded sweatshirt with blue jeans and had shoulder-length blonde hair. When I shared with her about how I identified her place by the decorations, she found it amusing and said, "it has just been who I am."

Heather spoke of how her parents seemed to just deal with and accepted their child's difference, which Heather referred to as being a "sissy." They took her to a therapist when she was about 9 years old. Years later, when Heather was collecting documentation for transition, she came across the transcripts from her childhood therapy sessions in which the doctor commented that she was the youngest transsexual he had ever encountered. She imagined the situation was heartbreaking for her parents in the 1960s and 1970s, taking their young son to a psychologist to see what they could do to help and being told their son was a little girl. At the time, there were few role models or representations to turn to for guidance. Heather noted, "There was no Jerry Springer, there was nothing. You know, there was Uncle Arthur on Bewitched but that was it . . . there was the tennis player, Renée Richards." There was also another male-to-female (**MTF**) transsexual in the town before her. When sh was in sixth grade theater, she recalled "seeing the most beautiful woman I have ever seen." That night she asked her mother about the beautiful "blonde-headed woman" who it turns out her mother knew, "but was kind of keeping her from me, you know. This wasn't like Boy Scouts and a pedophile. This was, oh God, we know if we get these two together it is going to start clicking, you know? And it clicked. It clicked."

While little help was available, Heather believed her father having a gay brother "cushioned the blow for him." She recalled:

> My uncle did not want to be a woman, but he was a big, you know, monocle-wearing brooch-wearing queen from Atlanta, so you know, thank God, he kind of cushioned that stuff a little bit but this was their child. This was sissy, you know, that kind of stuff, so I think that is hard on parents. I think any kind of thing that happens to your child, you don't want them to hurt. You don't want them to be in pain. It really wasn't that painful and hurtful when I was a kid. I mean, you know, sissy. It is not like, well, maybe it is like what happens today but I just think this bullying stuff is just taking it to a whole other level. If I could get called a sissy, fag, and queer once a day, really? Just move on with it because it does affect you, but then you have to compartmentalize what is going on and just realize that when you went to school it was going to happen and then when you went home you were in your safe place and that is just kind of how I dealt with it.

As difficult as life was at times, and as challenging as her identity may have been for her parents, Heather clearly viewed her childhood home as a safe place to be herself. And although her father had passed away by the time of our meeting, Heather kept in regular contact with her mother who lived about an hour's drive away. Of her mother she said, "She is great . . . we have always had a good relationship, but it is just good to have a mother-daughter relationship. I would not have had it the other way."

Heather also had two siblings, a brother and a sister, with families of their own. She was not as close to them as she was her mother, but noted that this stemmed from geographical distance and busy lives, not from her trans* identity. She saw her siblings and nieces at holidays and loved the time she got to spend with them, they just lived different lives.

Mothers are an important part of many people's lives and much like Heather's mother was for her, Maya described her mother as, "my best friend." Maya, a 26-year-old Black trans* female, grew up in the southern United States and openly acted as an advocate for the trans* community. She also had paid employment in the hospitality industry, worked as a hairstylist, and competed in the pageantry ball scene. I originally met Maya through a mutual friend, then interviewed her for this project a few months later. When I met Maya at her apartment, I had the opportunity to see her in a more comfortable, casual setting. Usually all made up, fashionably dressed, and flawless, seeing Maya at ease at home I noted, "she was wearing a purple hoodie and black sweat pant Victoria Secret Pink set."

In addition to maintaining a good relationship with her mother, Maya put in time, effort, and care with her maternal grandmother as well. Maya's maternal side of the family was Haitian and she noted that her transition was "a big culture shock" for her maternal grandmother. Because of this, Maya took a month and a half one summer to go spend time with her grandmother in Atlanta to show her grandma that she was still the same person. She gave her grandmother an opportunity to observe that her personality had not changed and that she remained the same "bubbly, witty, snappy" personality. She explained her transition as:

> Just like a woman who was a child who grew up. I just grew up. When we're younger, we have certain things

about us and those things evolve. That's exactly what it is. It's not necessarily a change, you're just evolving from who you were.

According to Maya, having gone and spent time with her grandmother to show her that she was growing up and still the same grandchild:

> sealed the deal right then and there. She's very strong in her beliefs in Christ and everything else. She loves me unconditionally and she just wants what's best for me. She's actually scared, she just doesn't want anything to happen to me or for somebody to harm me.

While some trans* people are never given the opportunity, being able and making the effort to show her grandma that she remained a good person made all the difference in Maya's relationship with her grandmother.

Unlike the entirely positive relationships Heather and Maya discussed, Donna's family experience covered a bit of both positive and negative reactions and spanned both family of orientation and family of procreation relationships. Donna, a 63-year-old, White trans* female introduced in Chapter Two, started transition at the age of forty-one. At the time of her transition, she was a parent to three children and had recently divorced from her wife of 20 years. Since transition, her mother, her mother's side of the family, and her sister all ceased communication with Donna. Recounting her relationship with her mother Donna lamented:

> My mother said some very hateful things. She then wrote me a letter with more and I was very, very hurt for quite some time. I did attempt to get in touch with my mother after about a year and phone calls got hung up, letters did not get answered and eventually, I gave up.

Just this year, I tried again and got nowhere and my mother's now 90 years old. I really would like to make some kind of connection but I don't think it's going to happen.

Donna noted that she and her sister had a strained relationship from an early age, so the loss felt less significant than with her mother.

As for the paternal side of her family, Donna's father died when she was in her twenties and an uncle had also passed away. In Donna's own words, her remaining uncle on her father's side, his wife, and their eleven children "surprised the heck out of me." A meeting with one cousin led to a conversation with the uncle's wife and a warm welcome overall. Given the difficulties she has faced in relationships with much of her family, Donna pointed out "that's been really nice having that group in my corner."

When it comes to family of procreation, Donna was only in contact with one of her three children: her oldest daughter. She knew that her other daughter lived across the country in the South and that her youngest child, her son, lived with his wife and children several hours away, but still in the Pacific Northwest of the United States. Like many trans* people, Donna "knew that it was a definite possibility that I would lose my whole family" and she had lost a lot. She recognized that although it is not the same, having the acceptance of her uncle's family has helped in dealing with so many family members cutting ties. In addition to her uncle's family though, Donna had been with her current partner for more than 10 years. Her partner also had children from a previous relationship and was Donna's friend before the two became partners. Before their relationship started Donna spent a good deal of time at her new partner's house and her partner's four children took well to Donna, creating what she called a surrogate family. She pointed out that, "If I hadn' had them, I would have survived but it wouldn't have been a comfortable."

Dating and Creating Families Post Transition

While some trans* individuals are in relationships with partners who support them and their transition in a variety of ways (Bishop 2016; Ward 2010), many trans* people do not experience relationships during transition so positively. Among the people I interviewed, only 13 percent were in the same relationships that they were in before transition. Some people were single when they transitioned, while for others, their relationship ended during the course of their transition. 87 percent of the people interviewed dated and formed new relationships from a new social position—both as a trans* person and with a different set of gender behavior expectations than they were held to prior to transition. In addition, they faced the challenge of deciding if and when to disclose that they were trans*-identified. Some had used disclosure as a weeding process—where, by telling people up front, they avoided investing energy in anyone who was going to have difficulties with it in the first place. Others waited to disclose, checking to see if a connection was likely in order to see if it seemed worth opening up to the potential vulnerability of that topic. Still others expressed concern that they should disclose early in order to avoid any appearance of an attempt on their part to deceive others. These fears have been fueled by defendants in court battles having used accusations of deception by trans* females to justify their violence up to and including killing trans* females (Lee 2006). As an initial example of approaches to dating as trans*, Charlotte discussed her own various approaches and those of people she knew.

I met Charlotte, a 41-year-old, White trans* female, at her home in Seattle. Her housemate answered the door and let me into the front room. Charlotte appeared, apparently from the kitchen, hands still wet from washing dishes. She was dressed in a long-sleeved white and black sweater-shirt with black leggings and had long sandy blonde hair. I noted that she was, definitely legibly read as female, with no question." After introductions, the housemate headed for another room and

Charlotte and I sat down together comfortably on a small beige couch to talk. She gave me her history of transition in a short, practiced form, indicative of having rehearsed this "elevator speech" over the course of many public speaking advocacy presentations.

When asked about when/where in her life her trans* identity still came up for her, having started medical transition 7 years before our meeting, she began with a story about a date she had gone on that week and her use of the online dating service "Awkward Cupid" as she called it. She mentioned that she, "wrestled back and forth with where do I disclose." She clearly had conversations with trans* friends about this very topic and informed me that some of her friends made their trans* identity clear in their profiles. Some of her friends did not disclose on their profiles, while others used a space near the end of the profile where one could list, "one thing I am not willing to admit but I am going to tell you anyway." Charlotte noted that, "other people will put it right at the top, the first sentence, 'by the way, trans*. Hey, you are still reading, good.'" She pointed out that she tried a variety of methods and settled on disclosing in an approach that was basically, "by the way I'm trans*, moving on, you know. It is about as interesting as me being a film maker."

Telling the story of the date she had, Charlotte explained:

I meet her at the bar and she knows I am trans* and she is great about it. We discussed it online and we talked and so I get to meet her for the first time, but I am meeting her friends who are there at Karaoke and they meet me and I don't know if they know, don't know if they do know, whatever, but they are like "oh, you have such a, such a rich robust voice. Are you a professional singer?" I am like, yeah, that explains it. That absolutely explains my rich and robust, you know. I've got this huskiness and they are like, "oh, I bet that is great, are you a singer, is that why?" I somehow, you know, I have exercised this particular muscle as a professional in some way that makes my voice huskier, or I'm more raspy. I don't know, I have no idea. So, you know, being able to explain myself jovially and conversationally without revealing too much, without lying. It's like how do I answer their question, while answering the question truthfully, while inveigling what they are probably . . . what they are really asking is what is the origin of your voice, and I am like I'm not willing to tell you that.

Although Charlotte discussed disclosure more from a standpoint of concern for whether people would still be interested once they found out, Nima spoke of a different concern—the fetishization of trans* females by (presumably cis*) males.

Nima, the 48-year-old multiracial trans* female introduced in Chapter One, saw herself as recognizably trans*, which made a difference in the dynamics of the dating scene. For her, disclosure was not a question of claiming a trans* identity or not in the way that it was for Charlotte. Instead of deciding whether or not to disclose right away and how that might influence dating dynamics, Nima found herself more likely to have to question the intent of the men who pursued her because her trans* identity was already visible. Were they interested in her as a human being on a deeper level or only interested in satisfying a sexual curiosity of their own? When I asked Nima about whether or not she was dating, she started her reply by first educating me about the realities of how trans* females, especially those who did not qualify for Whiteness, were often approached by males. Nima explained:

This is the thing, trans* women tend to be very sexualized by men. And there are a lot of men, heterosexual men . . . and the reason I say heterosexual is because these men identify in the heterosexual world as heterosexuals, their socialization is in mainly heterosexual world or society. But they're attracted, there's something about a trans* woman, the duality of a trans* woman, that attracts them. That doesn't mean they don't like . . . biological women. But they still have a taste, a sexual attraction, for a trans* woman. Often times because they identify as heterosexual and their lifestyle is heterosexual, they are not comfortable being open about the fact that they're attracted to transsexual women, the fact that they see transsexual women or the fact that they even date transsexual women. So what happens for a lot of us is that our relationships end up being very singular to the mistress-type relationship. Where they're only calling you in the wee hours of the morning, it's very under-the-cover-of-dark type vibe, very secretive. You don't get the dinners out or the movies because they don't want to be seen with you in public. They're afraid of how people are going to react and if their secret is going to come out.

Nima also talked about how a male's concerns about his family impacted his relationships with trans* females. She suggested that nine times out of ten, the men had a wife or girlfriend at home who was a cis* female, "but then they want to step out and explore and have a little play-time with us." All of which was to explain the difficult dynamics involved in relationships for many trans* females interested in dating cis* males. She noted that sexuality was often the primary focus, rather than a relationship per se, which made these encounters feel very "one dimensional." Nima stated, "You find yourself only hooking up, only getting together when the guy wants to, you know, have a sexual experience. So it can be pretty difficult." She also noted that, "there are guys out there that love us, oh yeah. There are a lot of them, but they're scared, in many ways to stand in their truth." She related:

I had a guy tell me once, if the world was different, our relationship would be a lot different . . . And my response to him is, sometimes you can't wait for the world to be different. You can't wait for the world, you have to do it anyway. Eventually the world will get on board, maybe. Maybe.

Even with all the potential problems, Nima had not given up, but she had become selective. She said:

> I'm open to dating but at this point, I don't have time for the bullshit. At this point in my life, I can do that all by myself. So, I'm open to it and hey, who knows. But, at the same time, I'm not just going to settle either. I think a lot of us, being trans* girls, we end up settling.

Coming from the very different perspective of trans* male identification, unlike Charlotte or Nima, Eduardo discussed disclosure of his trans* identity more as a matter of family creation. I interviewed Eduardo, the 36-year-old self-identified Chicano trans* male from Chapter Three, at his parents' home in a nice, newer construction subdivision of a small town on the west coast, outside of the Bay Area. At roughly 6 feet tall and 280 pounds, his size, let alone the effects of hormones, made him unlikely to be viewed as trans*. According to my notes, Eduardo "was dressed in black slacks, a nice black button down, black dress shoes and had white spats on" as he was heading out for a date at a speakeasy-style club after the interview. It was going to be his second date with the woman and he had not yet brought up being trans*.

Eduardo and I discussed the pros and cons of when to disclose a trans* identity in the dating process. I pointed out that on the one hand, saying something early could be a filtering process and end relationships with people who would not accept a trans* partner, before getting emotionally invested. On the other hand I mentioned that, "sometimes the most transformative moments for people are when they get to know somebody on a personal level first and that is not like the only thing they know about you, right?" Eduardo noted that he usually waited until a second or third date for precisely the latter reason. He responded:

> I want her to find out who I am and what I do for work, what kind of sports I am interested in, you know, family, my hobbies, what I like to do and then if you jive and you accept all those things and I am cool and you like me and you still want to hang out with me, then there is this other thing that you really have to get past.

As for the potential of trans* identity disclosure weeding people out early, he explained there was a way to go about sorting without mentioning being trans*. He shared:

> I tell them about the fact that I can't have any children, at least not personally. I tell them we could adopt, we could have other ways but I can't give you children, and that . . . can weed out women because I am 36 years old right now. Most of the women I am dating are in their 30s and they are all ready. If they haven't had kids already, which I usually tend to date women who don't have children, they either want one or they may not at that point, and most of them want one, you know. So that is one of the, what do you call them? Deal breakers. It is hard because you want them to know you and yet balance that with when to tell them.

Eduardo had not yet had genital surgery, though was planning to do so, and believed his disclosure strategy would likely change after surgery. Still, he noted that even after surgery, there would still have to be a conversation about the possibilities surrounding having kids. Over the years Eduardo found that for him, dates were "more accepting, if it is a medical condition . . . but not so much that I purposely went out and started changing physica characteristics to basically adapt to my body or how I feel on the inside."

Trans* identity was not only an issue of disclosure, such as when it came to choosing a partner with shared ideas and desires around creating families, or needing to think about the possibilities for family formation. Brad and his partner were already raising a child and had to consider the legal parenting rights and responsibilities concerned with being trans* and whether one was legally classified as male or female.

When I met Brad, a White 34-year-old trans* male, he was living with his wife of more than 10 years and their 4-and-a-half-year-old son, to whom she had given birth. I observed:

> [Brad] has reddish-brown long curly hair that he pulled back into a ponytail, showing that the sides were shaved. He also wears a mustache and really full beard. He was wearing casual cargo shorts and a short-sleeve button down shirt in a light green/blue plaid I believe. It made sense that he works at a food co-op as his attire, tattoos, and demeanor gave a hippie-crunchy queer vibe.[5]

Important to Brad's story was that he was living in Florida, a state that did not recognize same-sex marriages, made adoptions difficult for same-sex partners, and Brad was still legally considered female. Brad and his wife had tried to put their son on Brad's insurance since it would be cheaper. While his insurance company's national policy was to cover same-sex partners and their children, the state's insurance subsidiary of the same company did not, due to state policies. Even though Brad and his wife had been legally married in another state, the state they lived in neither allowed same-sex marriage nor recognized same-sex marriages performed in states where they were legal. Because their son was on the autistic spectrum, insurance coverage was even more crucial than it might have been for many other families.

Brad told me they had considered second parent adoption, but he would soon be getting his documentation changed, making him legally male. At that point they would be able to simply go get married again, which would automatically make him a stepparent. He likened it to the different reasons for name change and the levels of difficulty associated with that. Brad explained:

> It is like name changing, do you want to pay $250 and change your last name for no reason, or oh, do you want to pay $25 because you got married and it makes sense to change your name. So why are you, we're going to put you through this huge rigamarole to adopt this other person's child or oh, okay, it is way cheaper and that totally makes sense because you married this person and you guys are opposite sex. It is like $5, get on down the road. They make it extremely difficult. I think I am getting to a point now where it will be less difficult and less expensive once these things are in place.

In one final issue related to dating and creating families, I asked interviewees not only about the legal ramifications of being a trans* parent, but also how a trans* parent decided to deal with disclosure in raising a child. I was able to gain some insight about this issue from Gavin, who had just adopted an infant with his wife 4 months prior to our interview. Gavin was a 32-year-old White trans* male and young professional in the behavioral sciences who was not openly trans* at work. It was not that he hid his trans* identity, it was more so that many workplace relationships did not feel deep enough or connected outside of work enough to him to warrant disclosing trans* identity. With family, however, disclosure was a different matter. All of Gavin's extended family was well aware of his trans* identity. In part due to geographical location and in part due to the nature of his work, it was unlikely that family knowing and co-workers not knowing would come into conflict. Having a child changed the relationship between work and family or public and private more broadly though. I acknowledged to Gavin that I was motivated by personal curiosity to ask about how he anticipated talking with his child about his identity in the future. My wife and I may be trying to figure out how disclose my trans* identity to a child in the not so distant future, so it seemed prudent to ask someone with the benefit of psychological training.

In response to my question about being open about his identity with his child, Gavin let me know that he and his wife already had discussions about how they would go about this. They agreed that their daughter would know throughout her life about her father's identity and they had already begun to provide information, "in sort of an age-appropriate way." Obviously at 4 months of age, their daughter was not yet processing this information in any way. The process of talking to her was important to Gavin and his wife, in part as a way to practice how to discuss these things later. Gavin explained:

> I think it was mostly for us getting in the process because you know, it is like, you know we are going to be open about obviously how she was adopted and obviously talking about race and things like this, I mean, she is mixed race, and we are both Caucasian so we really want to talk about these things all the time. So I think I almost start to have these conversations with her even though she cannot understand just because I am starting to iron things out and how do I talk about this stuff and in an age-appropriate way? So I think I will just be saying like, you know, some girls just feel like they are much more male or whatever, or you know, want to transition, that sort of thing, and explain that to her I think. And I am sure as she ages she will just have more questions or I will give more information, but it is something that we want her

to always know, just like we are not going to tell when she is 13 that she is adopted, we are not going to tell her that I am trans*, right? It does not quite make sense.

Much like other identities such as being adopted and being multiracial, Gavin and his wife viewed having their daughter know about him being trans* as important. However, this did cause some anxiety about how her knowing would affect the private/public divide of who did and did not know Gavin was trans*.

Connecting Sexuality

As I discussed in Chapter One, within the United States, sexuality is generally defined as heterosexual, homosexual, or bisexual on the basis of the sex (female or male) of the individuals involved. This categorization structure also requires that both individuals have a binary sex, rather than being both or neither female and male or some other category of sex. While there are other terms for the labeling of a person's sexuality, this mainstream hetero/homo/bi construction has no option for those who have both breasts and a penis or a vulva and pectorals.

Sexuality is generally considered a separate identity and concept from either sex identity or gender identity. However, because we rely on sex (or sex category in making attributions of others) to categorize someone's sexuality, a trans* person's categorization label may easily change in the process of transition—even if their object of desire does not. Thus, someone who was assigned male at birth and desired romantic relationships with females would have been categorized as heterosexual. Once they have transitioned to female, however, they may be categorized as lesbian. For some, this change in categorization without a change in the sex category of the type of people they desire causes anxiety and hesitation about recognizing one's own trans* identity.

In an earlier research study (Seeber 2013) I met Roger, a trans* male in his thirties living in Seattle, Washington. Roger grew up in a homophobic, strict, Christian household. As a child, he knew that he was sexually attracted to males. In order to come to terms with the idea of his own trans* identity, he had to overcome his homophobic upbringing because becoming male also meant being a gay male. He explained that meeting the lesbian mothers of a past boyfriend had helped him move beyond his early beliefs and allowed him to recognize and accept his own trans* and gay male identity. He described his change in view of gay and lesbian people as it related to his own identities:

> I mean they were culturally aware and competent and they were warm and loving and I thought oh, so everything that I've ever heard about gay people is not right. And that's when I really, some light bulb started going off that I don't have to feel as angry and wrong as I do. I don't have to feel sick.
>
> (Seeber 2013: 40)

While some trans* people go through changes in categorization without changes in desire, some trans* people experience a change in who they desire (females, males, etc.) during the course of transition. There are at least three ways in which this may understandably occur. First, people's attractions may change over the course of a lifetime, whether they are trans* or cis*, as is discussed in literature about **sexual fluidity** (e.g. Diamond 2008; Rupp 2012).

Second, gender norms in the United States impact relationship dynamics in a number of ways. For example, someone assigned female at birth may find themselves attracted to females and males. However, they may feel uncomfortable with the role individual potential partners and society expect of them if they are in a relationship with someone male—the expectation of femininity, for example. That discomfort may then lead them to pursue relationships only with females because we, as a society, expect that relationship dynamic to look different in terms of division of labor, power structure, etc. While same-sex relationships may have additional stigma, there is often an expectation that the same-sex relationship will be more egalitarian. Eli, a 40-year-old White trans* male introduced in Chapter Two, spoke about his experience with relationships as an issue of dynamics. He explained it this way:

> Even the whole trying to be a lesbian thing was weird. I remember when I first came out . . . my best friend was like, "Really aren't you attracted to guys? Because, like, you had boyfriends." I remember really clearly saying, it's not that I'm not attracted to guys, I just can't be in a relationship with a man as a woman. Even though I had no concept of being in a relationship with a man not as a woman or what that would look like, but it's that dynamic that doesn't work for me. This like, no. It's better to just be with women because that's a better dynamic.

When that same individual assigned female at birth and attracted to females and males transitions to male, the expectations of individual partners and society change. Now the expectation becomes that relationships with males will be more stigmatized, but also more egalitarian. This dynamic change may make the possibility of pursuing relationships with males a more comfortable option than prior to transition.

Finally, it is not just the feeling of the relationship dynamic and expectations that can change in the process of transition There is also a transformation in the physical sensation o intimacy as one's body changes. It physically feels different t lay one's flat chest against a flat chest than to lay one's breasts against a flat chest. Similarly, changes in one's genitalia lead to a very different physical sensation against and with another's body. These variations in sensation may contribute to realizing sexual attraction to people of a sex category one had not previously explored.

Interpersonal relationships as discussed here regarding families, dating, and sexuality are significant issues in everyone's lives. However, trans* identity can contribute to a host of added challenges in these areas throughout a trans* person's life. In the following chapter I shift from the intricacies of personal and often private relationships to the more public issues of employment and housing.

DISCUSSION QUESTIONS

1. Imagine a significant event in your life: a new relationship, high school graduation, competing in a championship for sports or music, going to college. Was your family supportive of this event in your life? Was their support important to how you felt about yourself?

2. Think about the components of a traditional date. For ideas, you might search traditional date ideas online. In heterosexual couples, who is supposed to do what? Who asks for the date? Who decides when and where to go? Who pays? What do females do to show their interest? What do males do to show their interest? Now imagine switching places in these interactions—so if you are male, imagine what your role would be as female (femininity) and if you are female, think about what would be expected of you if you were male (masculinity). How easy or difficult do you think it would be to interact with a potential or existing partner in this new way?

3. What is something you feel is really important to who you are, but might not be visible to others? How do you handle

letting others know about this if they are or might become a regular part of your life, such as a close friend or dating partner?

Notes

1. I personally knew someone who experienced the bible-in-the-closet approach to the "correction" of her identity as lesbian.

2. In the U.S., while a few organizations and public events predate the 1970s, the movement for gay and lesbian rights is generally marked from the Stonewall Riots in June of 1969, while even the *term* transgender did not gain traction until the 1990s (see Valentine 2007).

3. Family of procreation is considered by some an outdated term as having or adopting children to raise is not a function of all families or partners (Benokraitis 2015).

4. Field notes October 27, 2013.

5. Field notes September 27, 2014.

5 Employment and Housing

There have been a couple of times where I was hired and assumed to be a cisgender woman, and later had some things that came up in my life to where . . . not that things came out but that I felt comfortable enough after being on the job for a couple of years to talk to someone that was in HR and tell them about my trans* experience, and then finding myself to be fired and unemployed after the fact. This was a place where I was promoted even before my 90-day probation period, and then after that, promoted twice and really was a really good employee, and had really good job performance. When I came out as being trans* to a certain individual, I was told that I would need to be psychiatrically reviewed before coming to work. At that time, our employee health insurance did not cover any psychiatric treatments or any type of psychotherapy and so I had problems paying for it. Then they fired me for not coming into work.

—Ryzha

Where and Under What Conditions We Work

Work is a central part of identity for Americans, including trans* people. Similar to females, discrimination, harassment and unemployment are particularly salient for trans* people. The *U.S. Transgender Survey* (James et al. 2016) garnered an impressive nearly 28,000 responses to their online survey over the course of 34 days during the summer of 2015. They found that among those who had been employed in the previous year, 30 percent had experienced some form of discrimination in the workplace during that year. 77 percent of employed respondents had taken one or more actions to avoid transphobic discrimination. Unsurprisingly, people of color faced higher rates of workplace discrimination and harassment (James et al. 2016). People I interviewed provided stories about difficulties with trans* identity in the workplace that covered a variety of challenges from finding employment to maintaining a job or career.

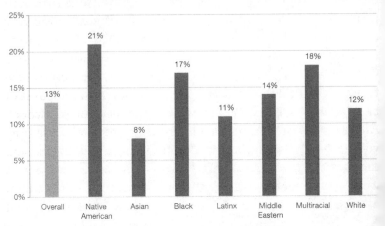

Figure 5.1 Ever lost a job because of being transgender by race/ethnicity (%), N = 27,715.

Source: U.S. Transgender Survey (James et al. 2016).

Walks With Two Spirits was a 57-year-old trans* female of Native American and French ancestry. She began her transition at the age of 16 and eventually left her small hometown in the South for big cities all over the United States, including San Francisco and Chicago. During the interview, Walks With Two Spirits wore reading glasses, a green shirt, and a long green skirt. Her long grey hair was pulled back into a bun. Having completed the GED for formal education, she had learned a great deal more from experience and doing the work than from reading books. She earned roughly $12,000 a year and did some volunteer work.

Walks With Two Spirits noted that at the time of her transition in the 1970s, there were very few job opportunities for trans* people, particularly trans* females. She recounted, "I mean I did find jobs. You know, I was pretty convincing at a young age. In the beginning, the jobs were, you know, you go to New Orleans, you put a dress on and you dance on stage." Not much had changed in the 20 years since the media drew attention to Christine Jorgensen, who also ended up in the entertainment business (Meyerowitz 2002). Walks With Two Spirits referred to the early days of her transition as "the dark ages" since at the time, visibility and medical treatment of trans* people were both pretty new and pretty scarce. She worked the clubs on the west coast, doing drag shows and strip shows, then moved to the middle of the country and found work at a Kentucky Fried Chicken as a female employee. Mostly though, she recalled how the options were "entertainment or sex work. That's about it or bar tending or whatever. Clubs, entertainment or sex work." After several years she shifted into social services work, including vocational counseling, food service at residential facilities, and the like. At the time of interview, Walks With Two Spirits worked in social services in a different town back in the south. She provided education and outreach around issues of HIV and AIDS and helped those living with HIV and AIDS.

Over the past couple of decades, job opportunities for trans* people, and particularly for trans* females, have changed somewhat, though many are still relegated to entertainment and sex work. Leddy, the White 45-year-old trans* female introduced in Chapter Two for example, earned a vocational degree that led to a well-paying, stable job. However, given her level of education and the ongoing workplace discrimination against trans* people, if she decided to leave the harassment and negative environment of her current employment, few opportunities would be available to her. Everyone at her place of employment was aware that Leddy was trans*. She transitioned on the job and stayed with the same company for 25 years. She explained:

> It would've been different if I'd left and got a job somewhere else but, no, I've actually hung out, fought it out and it's come with a heavy price. It has not been all easy, but I look at how many people today don't make what I make. People that are far more educated than me don't make my money and to work in the industry, a lot of hurt, a lot of pain, anguish and everything but it pays good. That's the other side of the coin is that I make a good living and it's getting worth it.

During the course of our interview, I noticed that Leddy had something of a "don't sweat the small stuff, and it's all small stuff" attitude that she also used as a strategy toward work. There were certainly things that bothered her about her employment and there were times when she talked about what other options might be out there for her. But her strategy was also a function of her reality. We talked about the job security she would continue to have from her job and demand for the type of work, so despite the stress of ongoing harassment and being passed over for promotion time and time again, she kept at it Leddy pointed out:

> If I left there, again, I'm almost 50. Nobody's going to want to hire me at this point because "A," I don't have a

college degree. I've got vocational school, and any more, at a minimum you need a bachelor's or something and even that, the friends and relatives that I know have college degrees would kill to make the money I make and so what am I going to do, go to Wal-Mart?

Leddy continued her story, explaining that not only did she make more than many people she knew with higher levels of education, she had a good deal more benefits as well. For example:

I started with the company a long enough time ago that when I started they were still doing pension plans. Even if I get fired tomorrow I still qualify for the pension so I will get a pension. I've also got a 401k, which was after the company had been bought up several times. The pensions went away, all the new guys, all they have is a 401k. I've worked for a big enough company that the retirement benefits are pretty good and I cannot imagine going anywhere ever again that I know that would have that benefit especially for somebody who really lucked into it. I'm stuck there. They realize that I'm probably not going to go.

So while there were times that Leddy contemplated leaving her employer to find a job with less ongoing harassment and obvious discrimination, she was pragmatic about her situation. She knew that unless it became a matter much closer to one of life or death she was not going anywhere. Her co-workers and supervisors knew this and made use of the knowledge to push the envelope of human dignity and respect.

Leddy paid dearly for the job stability and benefits she received, but her situation was in some respects better, or at least less precarious than Riley's. I drove out to the cornfields in the middle of nowhere to meet with Riley, a 49-year-old, White trans* male, in Wisconsin. I had driven a significant distance to get there, which made gauging my timing difficult. I ended up reaching town about an hour early, so I went to find food and ended up getting a sandwich at a Subway. In the process, I got stuck on an adventure trying to find my way back out of town because of a homecoming parade. So even though I had arrived in town early, I ended up getting to Riley's a few minutes late. Of course it did not help that the GPS on my phone ran out of information about a half mile to a mile before I reached his place. As I said—middle of nowhere.

Riley answered the door of his small farmhouse wearing a t-shirt with the name of a nearby college, well-worn blue jeans, and tennis shoes. He was in the process of making fresh spaghetti sauce and told me that his neighbors have a mill to throw whole tomatoes in, which removes the seeds, core, and skin, leaving the tomato pulp for sauce-making. It reminded me of being at my grandparents' place each summer in rural Oregon, canning and putting away fruit and vegetables for use during the winter. Oddly enough, while talking after our interview I found out that Riley actually knew where Mosier, Oregon (population less than 500) was. We chatted comfortably about rural life, where keys are often left in the car so they are easy to find. He told me he had a key to his house, but had never used it. Sometimes he went home to find a note from a neighbor who had come over and borrowed what they needed.

After hearing the overall research question and looking through the list of possible areas of life where trans* identity might still come up, Riley started with the issue of work. He noted:

> Certainly, you know, it's a work issue for me because I have to be closeted at my work. I don't have an option about that, although I did have the choice whether or not to take the job of course, knowing that ahead of time, and I work for a private, religious-based institution that you know, would fire me if they knew.

Riley had transitioned during graduate school and taken his current job knowing the risks, which included openly trans* people being prohibited as employees. In part he managed those risks by living a significant distance from his place of employment to help ensure that his professional and private lives never intersected. Given the importance of his faith identity, this gap between work and home also helped alleviate any issues that might arise from having to lie about where he went, who he spent time with, or what he did outside of work. Instead, he could simply be vague about many things, including the reason for my visit—helping someone with an academic project. While he noted that at times he wished he did not have to be "very evasive," or expend energy trying to manage a trans* identity at odds with religious life, in some ways life in academia was easier than in other jobs he had held. True, his employment was contingent on concealing his trans* identity, but this was much easier in an academic setting than say, traveling in cramped quarters and trying to manage being trans*. In Riley's case, the prohibition on being open about his trans* identity was explicit, while for others, like Ryzha discussed later in this chapter, negative consequences for coming out were more of a surprise.

Finally, in dealing with the options and conditions of employment, both Eduardo and Alex talked about how their identities mattered when working in dangerous environments. Eduardo, introduced in Chapter Three talking about the impact of racial identification, worked in the criminal justice system. He explained his work environment as follows:

> I work with the scum of the earth. I work with rapists, child molesters, murderers, sexual assaulters, men who commit domestic violence against their partners, their wives, bank robbers, I mean the worst of the worst of these people, and the mentally ill, the alcoholics, the drug users; these are my clients. I have been working there for 9 years

now . . . I have seen almost everything under the sun from dead bodies to piles of drugs, to whatever you want to call it; even burnt bodies, autopsies, a lot of stuff, you know. Gangsters, I mean working with these gang members, and I am not out at work. I am just Eduardo and no one would ever guess about my past, you know. I have told my supervisor. I had to go through a background check to be able to have access to every prison in the state . . . and every jail facility from here and up and down the coast, so I have to have clearance through the FBI and the Department of Justice as well and so everything was completed legally as far as my name change. My degrees have all been changed, driver's license, social security, passports, everything is under Eduardo, but I did tell my boss in case anything came up in the past that she would question me about, you know.

Eduardo did have a few colleagues who knew about his trans* history, but because of the potential risks involved with the type of work he did, eduardo noted, "the clients i work with, they don't get to know, and it always worries me that they may find out."

Alex, also introduced in Chapter Three discussing the implications of race, held a different type of trans* identity from Eduardo, but because he worked in a similarly dangerous environment, she was cautious about clients at work finding out about his trans* identity. When I met Alex at his apartment she was "wearing a faded black crewneck sweatshirt and dark blue jeans rolled up at the bottom." He was pretty small in stature, and noted that this made a difference in how she was treated, particularly when being perceived as male by others. Alex noted, "I work as male and I play sports as female." This was made possible in part because Alex was readable as either male or female. She took testosterone off and on for a time, the stopped several years ago, had a breast reduction down to nearly nothing, and then had some breast regrowth.

In the context of the queer community, Alex was very open about his identity and was out in her activist work. In his "day job," however, personal information was withheld as a matter of standard practice. In Alex's case, it was also withheld as a matter of safety. She explained:

> I work as male. I'm out to my clinical co-workers. The other social workers who are sort of mandated to be kind of progressive. Clients, absolutely not, no way. I work with a very severe population and it would not be safe. It would be destructive to any therapeutic relationship. I don't want them to know anything about me.

Because clients were in crisis and often violent and/or psychotic, being perceived as simply male was a strategy for Alex's safety and for effective working relationships. People being unable to sex categorize someone as either male or female could have created difficulties as discussed in Chapter Two on embodied capital. In addition though, given the situation of clients in crisis, the focus needed to remain on the clients and their needs, so the less information about Alex that entered provider-client conversations the better.

Stay or Go: "Status" Checks and Employment History

David, the White trans* male introduced in Chapter Two, noted that when he first decided to come out, he received top-down support from corporate headquarters who, "came in and told everybody if they discriminated, they'd fire them." David's positive experience at work meant he was able to retain stable, high paying employment and did not have to worry about the potential issues that might come with trying to find a new job.

Staying put was not an agonizing decision between a strained work environment and the possibility of discrimination in the hiring process for a new job based on one's status with respect to (trans*) sex, gender, and race. David also did not end up worrying about being **outed**, meaning having someone else disclose his identity as trans* without his permission, in a hiring process. This was a serious possibility whenever professional references were checked in what I refer to as **"status" checks**. David instead highlighted the best-case scenario of how an employer could handle a workplace transition—providing guidance from the top that clearly supported an employee living as their authentic self. On the opposite end of the employment environment spectrum, Ryzha was not given even the distressing choice between two less than perfect options.

I met with Ryzha, introduced in this chapter's opening quote and Chapter One, a mid-thirties Black and Native American trans* female, in the entry-room of a two-bedroom apartment near the coast in Miami Beach, Florida. She was crashing with a friend, being temporarily technically homeless at the time. She was dressed in cutoff jean shorts and a coral camisole tank. She had set out chairs in the entry-room for us to talk in the humidity and heat, which I referred to in my notes as "puddled air." Ryzha had attended college for a time at a small college in the south, although not because it was the most prestigious institution. She had been accepted at Harvard, but the other school offered a complete financial package, which she took for the "the level of independence that would afford her to explore her authentic self." Ryzha met such significant discrimination obstacles at school that she attempted suicide, was placed in a psychiatric facility, and ultimately was forced out of school.

Ryzha transitioned in her early twenties and had lived for a time in New York City. While in New York, she worked for a "multi-million-dollar nonprofit" in the Post 9/11 era. She explained how her trans* identity came up in the course of her employment:

In New York, I had an ID that did state that I was biologically female. When I applied to and went to jobs, being trans* wasn't really something that . . . that I had felt that I needed to talk about or come up with. Just like someone perhaps being biracial. You don't really announce for your ethnicity or what other race or culture that your family came from, because it didn't really apply to your job performance and to your job.

As noted in the opening quote, Ryzha was hired as female and later, feeling comfortable enough to do so, disclosed being trans* to someone in the Human Resources department. Shortly after, she was fired. By asking further questions I found out that not only had the firing come as a surprise after 2 years of service, Ryzha had been promoted before her 3-month probationary period had ended and promoted twice more before being fired. After coming out, she was told she would be required to take a psychiatric evaluation before returning to work. Her company health insurance did not cover such an evaluation at the time. Unable to come up with the cost out of pocket and unable to return to work without the evaluation, Ryzha was fired for not returning to work. I restated my understanding of what she said happened as, "Let us set up a trap for you and then we'll catch you in it," to which she responded, "exactly." All I could say was "wow."

Given the clearly discriminatory nature of Ryzha's loss of employment, her firing brings up another important issue for trans* people and work, namely the risks of discrimination in trying to find new employment. Ryzha had 2 years of work experience with the company before being let go. However, claiming that experience and garnering work references might not have been a possibility moving forward. Ryzha would have had to either risk the disclosure of her trans* identity from her previous employer, hope a new employer would be sympathetic to her situation and disclose being trans* in the hiring process, or lose the work experience by not reporting it. Ryzha went on to find employment through her LGBTQ connections at a place where her trans* identity was viewed as an asset.

The consequences of employment difficulties may also affect a trans* person's ability to medically transition, which in turn impacts employment opportunities, as Red's story explored. Red had to get creative to come up with the funds to transition. In my interview notes I mentioned that when I met Red, a 42-year-old White trans* female, she was "dressed in khaki green cargo shorts and a scoop neck green t-shirt." Red had long blond hair and I wrote that she was not visibly recognizable as trans*. At the time of our interview, Red had no job, no income, and was living at a friend's house in Tallahassee, Florida for the time being. Red first attempted to start transition in the early 1990s, but found that "it didn't last long. I only did it about 2 years and I could not get a job. I could not get the money. That just was not happening, so I had transitioned and then I had to reverse my transition." At the time, her transition had only included dressing in feminine attire and the occasional use of hormones, without any lasting bodily effects of hormones. With few prospects and no financial ability to medically transition, Red explained, "I went into the military 'cause I wanted the GI bill." Through the GI bill, Red earned an associate's degree in engineering and landed "a really good job." She started transitioning again, beginning with feminine dress, in the late 1990s and shared "of course I got fired right away."

Red found herself unable to find gainful employment for a second time as a result of starting her transition and being visibly recognizable as trans*. This time Red got creative rather than back-tracking on how she presented herself to the world. She found a cheap apartment just over the United States-Mexico border and looked for work on the U.S. side, crossing back and forth for work and sleep. She eventually managed to scrap together enough for medical modifications to her body. As she recalled:

I ended up getting enough money together, by what I had saved by living extremely frugal. I'm talking extremely frugal, like eating weeds on the side of the road. And I still do it, I love them. I mean I just really got to the point where if I could cut my food, I did. Where if I could not drive, if I could cut gas, if I can, you know, whatever I can do to save up that money, it didn't matter what it was.

Red pointed out that while some methods might have been questionable to others, "I wasn't gonna rob anybody or kill anybody or anything like that." Having reached a point where she felt her two options were to move forward with transition or kill herself, Red did whatever she could to get by and saved everything possible to fund the hormones and surgeries she needed to survive. In the early 2000s, Red managed to pay her way to Thailand for "the sex change surgery." After reaching a point where she was no longer seen as trans*, Red was again able to begin piecing together employment as an engineer, though she still faced sex discrimination as a female in a predominantly male occupation.

Penny's employment story was similar to Ryzha and Red's in the sense that transition had a negative effect which she had no control over. However, having more resources to begin with made for a different long-term outcome. Like Red, Penny transitioned in the early 2000s, but had far more resources at her disposal than did Red. I met Penny, a 56-year-old, White trans* female, at her home in a condominium complex. Casually dressed in a bright pink t-shirt, light blue jeans, and light brown fleecy boots, Penny had shoulder length brown hair and a deep voice. As we sat down in her living room to talk, I noticed two open computer towers in the middle of having hardware repaired on her desk and a server rack she had built in her front room. I noted her admission later in our conversation that her friends had often commented on how her place looked a bit too much like a bachelor pad and thus she was trying to hide some of the tech stuff to make it a little less manly in appearance."

At the time of her transition, Penny was working for a government-run utility company where she lived in the Pacific Northwest of the United States. She said that initially when she started the yearlong "**real life test**"[1] her employer was "sort of supportive. I was the first person to [transition] there. I had to teach them what to do." Penny also travelled out of the country to undergo surgical transition and said, "the transition went fairly well." She ended up having difficulties with her job at the utility company and received a blank piece of paper as a "personal improvement plan," meaning that "It didn't matter what I did better in, they were getting rid of me in 90 days." Penny noted, "I lost my job but, the benefits they gave me were really good." While she was shown the door in a similar fashion to Red, Penny had already secured enough sex category embodied capital to find new employment as female. Penny found work in the computer technology industry within 3 weeks of losing her previous employment. Her new employer was much more welcoming of all kinds of diversity. Penny also had work history to report, having been at her job much longer by the time she transitioned and was fired than Red. Penny listed her work history with the utility company and had no idea whether the new employer checked her references or not. After 5 or 6 years with the tech job, she had built a new list of references to work from by the time she needed to search for new employment again. By the time I met Penny, she was working as a software developer making roughly $120,000 per year. When asked about how social class had affected the challenges she faced and the resources she had for managing those challenges, Penny shared

> I've got a really good income. That does make it easier. I can socialize with well-educated people. It makes it easier to not have to run into issues and I've noticed a lot of pain and stress among trans women who don't have those

resources or trans women of color. I feel very fortunate in that regard. My life would be easier if I wasn't trans. But, you have to own who you are.

One final challenge trans* people might face with employment history and the possibility of reference checks has to do with the expectations employers have for employment and promotion trajectories. Imagine that someone assigned female at birth enters the job market as a female in a stereotypically female field, such as elementary school teaching. If the individual transitions to male and chooses to list their employment history and risk being outed in the reference checking process, questions may arise about promotions and employment level. As Williams (1995) pointed out long ago in *Still A Man's World: Men Who Do Women's Work*, instead of experiencing a **glass ceiling** in employment, males working in stereotypically female fields benefit from a **glass escalator**. Williams (1995) noted that males working in these fields were promoted very quickly to upper administrative positions—like rising through the ranks on a glass escalator. By contrast, our hypothetical female-assigned, now viewed as a male elementary school teacher has likely been promoted at the speed of other females.

A potential employer looking at this individual as male is likely to look at his work history with male promotion expectations. This means the employer would expect that based on the number of years our trans* person has been employed as an elementary school teacher, he should have long since been promoted to principal at an elementary school or beyond. The trans* person's lived experience as female and promotion path as female are then at odds with the hiring employer's expectations of male promotion history. This can easily reflect poorly on the trans* person in an employer's eyes. Having only been promoted as far as a female would have been, but appearing male, a potential employer is likely to wonder if there is some personal failing in the potential employee that accounts for having been promoted so little. This works against the trans* person in future employment possibilities.

Listing work history can mean the trans* person risks appearing to be less than an ideal worker based on their promotion trajectory, but not listing that history is likely to be worse. Not only does a lack of experience in a particular field mean starting at entry level employment, the trans* applicant also has the disadvantage of trying to explain the lack of history. Females re-entering the labor force after many years of raising children find themselves having difficulties securing jobs. How does someone apparently male in a culture that expects females to do the childrearing and caretaking, explain a long gap in employment? What would be a reasonable explanation? In addition to the risks of being outed as trans* in the process of reference checks then, trans* people face discrimination based on the sexist expectations of employment and promotion history.

Trans* people find themselves caught in a web of difficulties when it comes to the world of work. Publications about trans* people in the workplace suggest that employers can help retain trans* employees and smooth their workplace transitions by providing top-down support like David received (HRC 2004, Weiss 2007). This support has long-term, positive consequences for trans* people in addition to the immediate effects on transition experiences. Remaining with an employer means increased employment stability and avoiding potential problems with references checks and work history by subsequent employers. When trans* people move from one job to another after transition, they have to weigh the importance of work experience against the likelihood of discrimination. Either they let the hiring employer know that previous employment may be under a different, specifically a gender-mismatched, name, or have to contact previous employers and hope they are willing to provide references without mention of the previous name or transition (Mennicke and Cutler-Seeber 2016). Even then, a promotion history that does not match expectations for their apparent sex category may hold them back. The more unstable a trans* person's employment, the more frequently that person has to face the experience versus discrimination dilemma. While supportive employers can help with work stability issues, individuals with lower socioeconomic status face significantly less job stability than those with higher status.

From this perspective, not only did David have more social and economic resources at the time of his transition than did Ryzha or Red, but because of those resources David will face fewer challenges related to his trans* identity over the entire course of his working life. Penny, on the other hand, was pushed out from her job with the utility company. However, having more resources and managing to find a welcoming environment quickly to build new references in, she experienced something less positive than David, but remained in more positive circumstances than either Ryzha or Red.

Housing, Status Checks, and The Intersection With Economic Capital

Jess, a 29-year-old, White, working-class trans* male, stood about 5'2", with greying hair and a full mustache and beard, wore dark brown glasses, a black A-shirt, and grey pants. I scheduled the interview with Jess to coincide with a conference I was attending in Nashville, Tennessee. Jess picked me up from my hotel "and drove about 10 minutes away to his house, parking in a dirt/mud spot in the yard clearly used as a parking space."[2] He and his female partner rented a one-bedroom apartment that had been created in the attic of a single-family house. Jess was the first respondent that pointed out that his trans* identity had affected his housing stability in a similar fashion to employment—through status checks.

Jess and his partner had only recently moved to the city, and while he had a bachelor's degree, he was working as a server in a restaurant and making less than $10,000 a year. Later in the interview he revealed that he had never made more than $15,000 per year at any employment he had held. Still, Jess had been on hormones for about 4 years and had chest reconstruction surgery 2 years prior to our meeting, in part thanks to some creative crowd-funding.

As Jess pointed out to me, those who rent housing commonly have to provide references when searching for new accommodations. In my personal experience, some landlords request housing information for as much as up to 5 years prior. Jess shared a difficult time in his life with respect to housing:

> I had this very old gentleman that rented to me. It was my first apartment when I lived on my own when I was 21 and his name was Charlie and he was old as dirt. I had a studio apartment and we had a really great relationship. I actually got laid off and I started my unemployment checks, which were measly. I was signing them over to him just to show him that I was trying, and he kept a log of how much money I owed him. He was even paying my gas bill and I told him I would pay him back. I got laid off like 4 months into my lease, too. I finished out the year and 2 months after that year ended I sent him my last check paying off everything and he wrote me a really lovely letter. He was like, "I am sorry you fell on hard times, you restored my faith in renting to young people. Thank you." And it was a really great relationship, but then when I wanted to use him as rental history I just told the person . . . I was about to rent from them and I just told them. I was like, so when you talk to Charlie, first of all he is very old so you have to talk slowly. He will try and talk over you on the phone; I gave them that whole spiel and also my name was Tara when I rented from him. I am transgender; that doesn't, you know. People usually, I don't get any problems. What I

explained to them please don't tell Charlie my name is Jess now; it is going to confuse him. Please talk to him as though my name is still Tara, but for future reference I prefer male pronouns and everything. I like to be as flexible as I can because it is already a challenge and I don't want to like, I don't want to be defensive. I want to be understanding.

Jess had a positive experience in renting from Charlie, but his story points out how housing can be an area fraught with challenges. In many locations, a renter's market is created by a high amount of housing availability relative to the number of people searching, where landlords are trying to keep their properties from sitting empty. However, in many urban locations, the opposite situation exists, where landlords have people lining up to rent and management can be more selective. This latter situation of a landlord's market gets exacerbated by conditions such as the housing market crash in 2006. During a time of rental housing shortage, minority groups, including trans* people, find themselves in situations of increased housing instability.

In the process of purchasing a home, a trans* person's identity as trans* is likely to come up during background or credit checking. This opens up an opportunity for discrimination even if a person is not visually recognizable as trans*. However, home ownership is a more stable, long-term housing situation than renting, meaning that those with higher social class status are likely to run into fewer instances where discrimination could manifest. Those who have lower socioeconomic status are more likely to rent than to own their homes. Because of this, those in lower social classes have higher chances of having to provide references and run a higher risk of challenges with housing as a result of being trans*.

In addition to the direct relationship between current social class and housing stability, employment and housing stability are also linked. Those with lower education and income generally have less stable work *and* less stable housing. Work instability and lower-skill, lower-wage jobs increase the likelihood of having to move to where employment is available. Alternatively, losing housing may be a result of lost work as shown by Red and Ryzha who both found themselves staying with friends after being fired. In either of these cases, those of lower social status are more likely to have to face the challenges of reference checks both to obtain jobs and housing.

In the United States, males and females who visibly belong to racial and ethnic minorities that do not qualify for Whiteness find themselves experiencing multiple forms of social discrimination and exclusion. **Structural or institutional racism**[3] can and often does result in unemployment and unstable housing as well as other class-based issues, and being trans* adds an additional layer of discrimination. At the time of the *U.S. Transgender Survey*, the national average for unemployment was at 5 percent, however, the rate for survey respondents was 15 percent (James et al. 2016). When broken down by race/ ethnicity, the reality was far worse for most trans* people who do not qualify as White. Black trans* people were unemployed at 20 percent and Native American 23 percent. Latinx and multiracial trans* people reported unemployment at 21 percent and 22 percent respectively. Those of Middle Eastern descent reported an alarming 35 percent unemployment (James et al. 2016). The situation was not much better with regards to housing. While almost one third of respondents had spent some time as homeless in their lives, 12 percent had been homeless within the last year alone, specifically because of transphobic discrimination. The rates of homelessness in the last year were higher for trans* females who were Black Native American, multiracial or Latina (James et al. 2016) Clearly being trans* contributed to employment and housing difficulties and these challenges were exacerbated by racism and sexism.

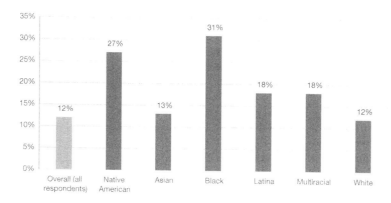

Figure 5.2 Homelessness in the past year because of being transgender among transgender women by race/ethnicity (%), N = 27,715.

Source: U.S. Transgender Survey (James et al. 2016).

In the following final chapter, I discuss difficulties trans* people face regarding dignity and care. Healthcare, eldercare, and end-of-life decisions can be difficult to negotiate or even contemplate in general, but stigma, incompetence, and discrimination make each of these areas that much more fraught with anxiety and concern.

DISCUSSION QUESTIONS

1. Conduct an online search for your school's student handbook or employer's employee handbook. Locate the non-discrimination policy and see if it includes protections against discrimination on the basis of gender identity, gender expression, and/or sexual orientation. Because these are the most explicit types of policies covering trans* and LGBTQ people from discrimination in the workplace, how would you go about suggesting and/or implementing these policies in your school or workplace?

2. Look up a website for a real estate company that operates in your area. See if you can locate a policy regarding non-

discrimination for the services they provide including renting and purchasing of housing. What protections does the company include in their policy?

3. How are issues with employment and housing also related to an individual's socioeconomic class? Why does the intersection of socioeconomic class with trans* identity make employment and housing more challenging?

Notes

1. The "life test," "real life test," "one year life experience," etc., refer to the criterion of living one year in the preferred sex/gender, which used to be required prior to being recommended for hormone therapy. In the most current *Standards of Care*, the year of experience is only listed as a requirement for genital surgeries and can be completed while using hormones to change the body's appearance (World Professional Association for Transgender Health 2012).

2. Field notes February 8, 2014.

3. Racism is "the belief that members of separate races possess different and unequal human traits" (Conley 2008) and supplies the justification for discrimination, meaning the unequal distribution of resources and rewards in a society. Discrimination happens on an individual level, for example when an individual poll worker refuses to provide a voting ballot to someone of racial minority status. Racist beliefs and discrimination on the basis of those beliefs also occur at the level of social structures and institutions, for example in the creation of laws requiring particular forms of identification in order to be provided a voting ballot. These forms of identification are unequally distributed across people on the basis of racial categorization, making the system itself a means of perpetuating unequal resources on the basis of racial categorization.

6 Healthcare, Eldercare, and End-of-life Decisions

I've had trouble getting health insurance, but that's about to change. I've had to pay a lot more for health insurance than I've wanted to because of the getting denied. I was denied for health insurance and then we had a way to get health insurance through the state where they supposedly pay for part of it. It meant that I had to buy more insurance than I actually wanted. I just wanted a high deductible policy and they didn't offer it. There's going to be a huge thing now with the Affordable Healthcare Act that you can't be denied at all. Of course, there's still that high deductible policies at least the cost will go down there.

—James

Healthcare

James, the trans* male from Lexington introduced in Chapter Four while talking about being cast out by his family, also revealed that he faced significant challenges with healthcare insurance. A little confused and assuming I must not have understood correctly, I followed up James's explanation and asked, "You were being denied because of being trans*?" To this he nodded, "mm-hmm . . . yeah. Hadn't heard that one before?" I explained it had occurred to me that many trans* people did not have jobs or the types of jobs that offered health insurance. Alternatively, I was aware of people who had health insurance, but trans*-related care specifically was excluded, which was often broadly defined to include care not related to transition itself. However, I had not previously contemplated someone being denied health coverage entirely on the basis of considering being trans* a *pre-existing condition*. Thankfully, at the time of this writing, insurance companies are no longer allowed to deny people coverage on the basis of pre-existing conditions—at least for now.

While issues of being turned away from healthcare on the basis of being trans* appear to be on the decline, access to informed, competent care still remains a difficulty for many trans* people. Issues around practitioner knowledge and having to "train" one's doctors remain significant challenges. Trans* people are more likely to find practitioners who are open to working with trans* patients today than in the past. However, open as they may be, doctors often do not necessarily have the knowledge and authority to guide and instruct. This lack of practitioner knowledge can contribute to trans* people's hesitation to seek medical care, particularly when traveling or relocating—when the likelihood of having to come out and train a new medical provider is at its highest. As Taye, a Black trans* male introduced in Chapter Two, noted:

> where it . . . affects me in unknown circumstances in health encounters. And so I got a good physician and I got a good network that I'm tapped into, but in cases where I'm in an emergency situation or I have to go to a doctor that I don't know or that's out of my network . . . then I get a little antsy because I've had few experiences with doctors and with people that were rude and disrespectful.

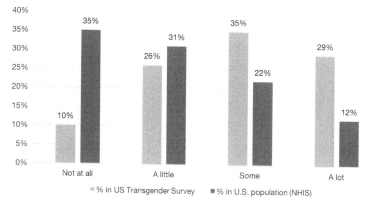

Figure 6.1 Interference of psychological distress with life or activities among those who reported feelings of distress in the past 30 days, N = 27,715.

Source: U.S. Transgender Survey (James et al. 2016; Centers for Disease Control and Prevention 2016).

Taye also pointed out, "When you're vulnerable and you're hurting . . . it's not always easy to push back at the system."

The issue of healthcare access is particularly pressing in light of scholarship that shows, for example, significantly higher rates of anxiety and depression within the trans* population than the general population (Budge, Adelson, and Howard 2013). Additionally, Allison Auldridge et al. (2012) noted that trans* people, and particularly trans* elders, face significant problems accessing healthcare and getting health insurance. The authors noted that this lack of accessibility is "due in large part to systemic discrimination from providers and insurance companies, as well as economic instability resulting from discrimination in employment and housing, among other areas" (Auldridge et al. 2012: 3). In these situations, trans* people are not only doing the work of providing medical knowledge, but also educating doctors and staff about how to provide identity verification for trans* people, for example, by referring to trans* people with preferred names and pronouns. At the same time, these patient/instructors are dealing with the high risk of being misidentified in initial interactions. Thankfully, groups such as the National Center for Transgender Equality are lobbying to get transition-related care covered.[1] However, the healthcare system in the United States still has a long way to go before trans* people's concerns about competent care can be put to rest.

Accessibility

I met David, a White trans* male from Chapter Two, at his home, in a middle-class residential neighborhood in Minneapolis. When filling out demographic information before the interview, he asked if he could simply enter "upper middle class" for his income, as he did not feel comfortable sharing that information. I would not be surprised if he made twice the next highest participant's income.

In the 10 years between when he first figured out he was trans* and when I met him, David had started hormones and had chest reconstruction and a complete hysterectomy in one surgery. He had also gone through three surgeries so far in his journey of genital reconstruction: **mons resection**, metoidioplasty, and urethroplasty.[2] Genital surgeries alone had cost him nearly $40,000 and a good deal of recovery time over the course of almost a year. David had one more lower surgery planned and shared "I suspect that in a number of years, I'll go and have a phalloplasty."[3] In addition to the cost of surgery itself, there are a variety of costs associated with medical modifications.

Time off of work is a financial burden for many and not all employers are willing or able to allow for the amount of time necessary for recovery. There are only a handful of surgeons in the United States performing transition-related surgeries, so there are also the costs associated with travel to a surgeon' location, including needing to stay close by for follow-up care David pointed out "I've got a job that will let me leave and go see the doctor," which is not necessarily a reality for many trans people. He also noted that for "most of the trans* guys that I've gotten to know, as is true with most of the population, spending $100,000 or $200,000 on surgery is just not a real practicality. I'm lucky. My insurance has covered everything except for travel and hotel." Insurance plans that cover transition-related medical care, particularly surgeries, are increasing, but are still few and far between. And even though insurance covered the costs for David, he still had to prepay for his genital surgeries and get reimbursed after, which required having the money up front anyway. It would take Jess, the 29-year-old restaurant server from Chapter Five, 4 years of income with no living expenses to come up with the funds that David paid up front. That would not even account for whether or not he could get the time off work or for the lost pay from being out for surgery and recovery. This makes metoidioplasty, let alone phalloplasty, in David's words, "just not a real practicality" for someone like Jess. Clearly economic capital has a significant influence on who can make the body they feel is authentically their own a reality.

Economically speaking, Noah found himself in a similarly challenging position to Jess. Noah, a 46-year-old White trans* male, earned only a small stipend for facilitating a trans* support group in a town in the Pacific Northwest and lived on less than $20,000 per year. When I met him at his small one-bedroom apartment I noted, "He was dressed in blue jeans and had a blue t-shirt on under a grey long-sleeved, warmer shirt. He has short, darker brown hair with a full, neatly trimmed mustache and beard." I also wrote notes to myself that "He is a bit shorter than me and more pear-shaped, though unless one was in a context where trans* people were expected, the facial hair and general appearance mean he is never viewed as trans*." Noah had been on testosterone therapy for approximately 8 years when I met him. He had managed to save up enough money for chest surgery about 3 years after starting hormones, "Thanks to my mom," according to him. Although he wanted to have genital surgery and started saving toward that goal, he mentioned, "at this point, I don't know if I'll ever be able to get bottom surgery." Given the financial considerations just discussed, his outlook was unsurprising.

As similar as their economic situations were though, there were social differences in the stories of Jess and Noah. Jess pointed out that he had access to more information than he would have otherwise by virtue of living in a college town, near the college, and having friends who were going to school. He shared:

> . . . they had resources through the university, which was a big deal. So I would say that I had questions and I could name five people off the top of my head from 7 years ago that told me immediately where I needed to go and where I needed to get started, and they knew these things because they had taken a gender/women studies class or they had a professor who talked about trans* issues.

Jess did go to college about 10 years after graduating high school, but at the beginning of transition, he relied on friends in college to provide him with access to reading material. Noah on the other hand, grew up with parents who both earned PhDs and there was no question he would attend college right out of high school. When asked about the influence of socio-economic class on his transition, Noah replied:

> I have to admit, being a more or less middle class, college educated, White male or apparent male, probably does get me a level of access that not everybody can necessarily count on. Being college educated, I have the vocabulary and the manner that I can usually get establishment figures, like doctors, to listen to me. Not everybody can claim that. The access issues are very different for women, including trans* women, people of color, poor people, people who don't have the educational background that I have. I guess I use the tools that I have and the hope that people beyond me will benefit somehow.

Noah's experience with doctors and "establishment figures" are the epitome of Annette Lareau's (2002) findings on the ways in which parents, regardless of race, pass on social class privilege to their children. She noted that middle-class parents teach their children "to be an informed, assertive client in interactions with professionals," like doctors (2002: 767). In contrast, in working-class and poor families Lareau noted that, "adults as well as children . . . tend to be deferential and outwardly accepting in their interactions with professionals such as doctors and educators" (2002: 749). This class-based distinction in doctor-client interactions can be particularly important when it comes to self-identity and transition-related care. Eli provided an example of the importance of assertiveness in particular.

Eli, first introduced in Chapter Two, was born and raised in a small European country. Although I met him in Berkeley, California where he was doing research for his master's degree, his stay was time-limited and he would be returning home to Canada, his place of citizenship. Eli's medical transition at that point had taken place in Canada, as would his future surgical plans, where transition related care could be covered by national health insurance. Surgical coverage was not guaranteed, however. Much like the gender clinic systems of the mid 1900s in the United States, the Canadian system was based on a particular understanding of what a trans* person's story should look like. This system also assumed a singular model of how medical transition should proceed: hormones, top surgery, genital surgery—in that order and from start to finish with all procedures included. Eli's story of desiring to move from a female body to a less female body, but without necessarily desiring to behave in a particularly masculine way at the end of it all, did not fit well with the expected female-and-feminine to male-and-masculine two boxes social system. Instead, Eli envisioned himself ending up being perceived as a "sissy guy" who had some combination of female and male genitalia.

When Eli started his medical transition, he sought out chest surgery first. He attempted to avoid the gatekeeping, one-trans*-

narrative assumptions of the sex/gender specialty doctors by seeking a breast reduction. He recalled, "At first I talked to them about doing a breast reduction because my breasts were big enough that it would be covered as a reduction . . . and I was like, basically I want a reduction, but to like basically gone." The surgeon informed him that they could only reduce him to a size C. The C cup threshold had nothing to do with medical standards and everything to do with beauty norms and cultural expectations about female bodies. This logic of "proper" female sizing was at odds with Eli's purposes for requesting reduction, however, and could potentially interfere with future chest plans. Eli explained:

> I knew that if I went through that surgery and then later was like, yeah, this is not enough then it made having top surgery more complicated because you already have scars and stuff. I'm like, okay, this is not making sense. I'm really going to have to go through the whole gender thing.

Eli went through the sex/gender, trans* specialists instead, but still had to fight and negotiate to get what he wanted because his narrative did not fit the model understood by the specialists. He was not yet on hormones and did not identify entirely as male, so while he was eventually approved for chest surgery, surgical funding was not approved and he ended up paying for it himself. Here, calling the expectation of binary sex category into question, what I discussed as the paradox of (trans*)identity in Chapter One, resulted in added costs for surgical body modification in a country where theoretically, it would have been free.

When I met with Eli, he was in the process of negotiating genital surgery. He originally went in asking for the clitoral release method used in metoidioplasty. However, he also specified that he did not want the surgeons removing or sewing up his existing internal and external genitalia, such as is done in **vaginectomy** and the creation of a scrotum from the labia majora.[4] Recognizing that the doctors were unable to understand a desire for anything not strictly male, Eli initially decided to simply go along with the doctors' understanding and get metoidioplasty with the expected vaginectomy. Before surgery was scheduled though, Eli found someone online who succeeded in ending up with something of both male and female genitalia in the way he also desired. Armed with the knowledge that this outcome was possible, Eli went back to the negotiating table about funding, having already found a surgeon willing to provide his desired genital outcome. He was still waiting to find out about whether or not his surgical choices would be funded when we spoke.

Initially in our conversation Eli attributed his ability to advocate for his desired body in contrast to his doctors' understanding of "trans*," to his maturity level. He explained:

> I think the fact that I was older when I transitioned actually helped a lot. I felt like with the doctor, like in terms of accessing medical stuff, both for my top surgery and now going through this process of having spent all that earlier time figuring out my shit and learning how to communicate with people helped a lot because I felt like that doctor particularly really wanted to push me in a particular direction and to be able to resist that I feel like having that kind of more maturity. Like if I tried to do that when I first thought of it when I was 23 or 24, I wouldn't have been able to navigate that system as well as I could.

Thinking through the history of his life as Eli had shared it with me, I asked if some of the self-advocacy skills were related to changes in his class status. He replied:

> I feel one of the things that really helped me actually was . . . the person I moved to Vancouver [Canada] with, she's [from where I was born] as well, but from a much higher

class background . . . I learned a lot about navigating systems from her and how to deal with people and communicate with them in a way that is quite alien to me . . . I've learned, I guess, *to pass as middle class in certain circumstances*, like to go and talk to the doctor in that kind of way and I learned a lot of that from her, which is a pretty valuable skill actually, even though I've been pretty broke for most of my life. But in that period when I was in a relationship with her I had more money than I probably will ever have again . . . I think it does impact in terms of even feeling the feeling of "I deserve that."

(emphasis added)

Without the assertiveness and the sense of deserving th treatment he sought, often learned in a class-based context, E may not have secured the medical procedures that met his specifi needs and provided him with a sense of authentic self.

Walks With Two Spirits also offered insight about wha passed as healthcare when she first started her transition in th early 1970s. She recalled:

Back then you would just go to a pharmacy and go in the back and tell them you want hormones. And the doctor would see you in the back and then you'd go to his pharmacy in the front and buy the hormones, then you're on your way. There was no blood draws, no exams. You know what I'm saying? You just were on your own. You get a shot in the butt, and that was pretty much transition.

Times had changed by the time I met Walks With Tw Spirits and she was getting her maintenance dose of hormon through a low-cost clinic in the historically segregated city i the south where she lived. Walks With Two Spirits also shed little light on how racial and ethnic identity intersected wit trans* identity in the healthcare arena. When asked about ho she felt race had or had not affected the challenges she had experienced in life, she offered this example:

> I come here and I get my hormone therapy. I'm White. I get my Premarin ... It's maintenance dose. I'm not expecting to transition anything else. Then there's a Black transgender. We're in the same kind of, I think there's 10 years difference. She's African American. She's castrated. The same agency from downstairs would not do her hormone replacement even though she was castrated and she needed some kind of hormone.

In addition to social class, racism clearly contributes to issues of healthcare accessibility.

Sex Coding and Insurance Billing

Charlotte, a White trans* female introduced in Chapter Four, discussed issues with having health insurance that stemmed from the complexities of trans* identity. She described how she had health insurance on which she was listed as male when she first began transition. At the time, she managed to find, "really sympathetic doctors that were ambiguous" about how they wrote things in her charts. She discussed how, "They were finding codes that worked that they could use to bill, but it was still a dance," so for some things, like hormones, she simply paid out of pocket rather than trying to deal with the hassle of insurance company questions. When she was further along in her transition she explained:

> Fortunately, when the new health plan came through, I was able to enroll as female without having to have a doctor's examination or anything. So that felt really liberating, to be able to get that female insurance, yet I knew

that there were still certain male elements. How do you explain a prostate exam, for example. So there were certain elements. How can you explain, you know, no pap smears at all, you know. Still, you go to the doctor and they still ask about pregnancy. "When was the last time you had your period?" I am like, uh, never!

Charlotte discussed how more recently things had become less challenging, but only because she had not had any health insurance for a while. She pointed out:

I am going to get some in January, yay "Obamacare."[5] I am ready to go through and figure out and fight the system if I have to, to get the care that I need in the way that I need it because even though "Obamacare" has made huge inroads, it is still completely ridiculous for trans* people. It is still virtually impossible to get the care that you need covered.

In addition to the challenges with coverage Charlotte shared with me, personal trans* friends have also shared similar difficulties. One friend was denied coverage for dermatological care because "transgendered" or "gender identity disorder" (GID) was listed as a secondary diagnosis on the insurance paperwork. So, while dermatological care is hardly "trans*-related" care, the insurance company denied the claim by calling it trans*-related. Such stories are disappointingly common in trans* communities.

Intersections of Health Exclusions: Between a Trans* Male's Legs

As Walks With Two Spirits' comments on getting hormone and the opening story of Chapter One about Nima and "pumping" attest, healthcare experiences are significantly impacted b intersecting identities. Lest we believe that the difference of race, class, and procedures are limited to trans* females, I turn to an exploration of the adventures abroad for genital surgery of Kevin, a Black trans* male introduced in Chapter One. Kevin's parents grew up in the poor, rural south, moved to a more populated area and both earned themselves doctoral degrees and a good living for their family with two children. Kevin grew up in the same relatively small city in the south where he transitioned and lived at the time of interview, earned a bachelor's degree, and made around $45,000 per year. When researching phalloplasty surgeons and costs, he found a few options in the United States ranging from $40,000 and $45,000 all the way up to $150,000. Since he paid for the initial surgery on his own, Kevin opted for a highly acclaimed surgeon in another country who was charging only $13,000—a country where few Black people were to be seen and hearing English spoken was uncommon.

Kevin described his surgeon as incredibly attentive, visiting him every day save one of the 26 days Kevin spent there. However, according to Kevin, the facility where his surgery took place "makes you feel like it's 1930 [sic] Cold War Russia. They use glass thermometers, glass syringes—things that just seem very antiquated." Kevin also pointed out that they did not use narcotics, but luckily someone else he knew had gone to the same surgeon and warned him in advance to bring things like pain, anti-nausea, and bladder spasm medication with him. After the more formal part of our interview, Kevin showed me pictures of his time abroad. When showing one of his hospital room he asked, "what's missing?" Then he pointed out the complete absence of machines—machines like monitors for heart rate, heart rhythm, and oxygen rate that we are accustomed to seeing in post-surgical hospital rooms in the United States. Not surprisingly Kevin said the route he took, "was not for the faint of heart."

Phalloplasty, or the construction of a penis, is a complex surgery that consists of multiple surgical procedures that may make use of a variety of surgical techniques, and is accompanied by a long period of recovery.[6] Kevin returned to the United States early because he was not recovering as well as his surgeon expected. Kevin attributed this to the stress of being in a new place without his family. Stateside though, it was discovered that Kevin had developed some necrosis on the tip of his penis that required a surgical revision. Although he was able to get the revision and aftercare he needed close to home, his insurance would not cover it. In addition to around-the-clock home care at their house, Kevin was lucky to have the financial support of his parents to cover the costs of the necessary treatment back in the United States.

Kevin considered himself lucky because although he acknowledged, "I've spent my life savings just now," he had far more financial resources than many trans* males, especially trans* males from oppressed racial and ethnic minorities. Despite the American Dream mythology and the idea that the United States is a meritocracy, class privilege and class mobility have always been structured by race and racism. However, there were additional difficulties for Kevin's phalloplasty that were entirely about race. Here I am not speaking about racism in the sense of negligent or biased treatment by individuals. Kevin generally spoke highly of the care, concern, and treatment he received from his surgeon and hospital staff abroad. What I am referencing here is at the institutional level—the distribution of knowledge and technology related to the skincare of dark-skinned people.

Kevin's surgeon told him that Kevin's was the first dark-skinned Black body on which he had performed this operation. As with any major surgery, phalloplasty results in a great deal of swelling and bruising. And because his surgeon was unfamiliar with dark-skinned bodies, it was difficult for Kevin's surgeon to properly assess the healing and condition of his transplanted organ. So while any trans* male with limited funds may look outside the United States for lower-cost alternatives for surgery because of the predominantly White/light-skinned population.

where these surgeries take place, the risks are lower for White trans* males opting for this route.

Trystan Cotten—professor, trans* male of color, and editor of *Hung Jury: Testimonies of Genital Surgery by Transsexual Men* (2012a)—pointed out that trans* males research and seek out genital surgeries for a variety of reasons. First, some recognize genital surgery as a necessary part of their authentic sense of identity and feeling whole, or what Cotten called "somatic congruence" (2012a: 2). Second, Cotten (2012a) pointed out that there are social bonding and intimacy experiences that may not be open to or do not feel safe for those without genital surgery. These included "locker rooms, showers, public baths, health spas, saunas, swimming pools, fraternities, the military, bars (including sex and strip clubs), and circle jerks, to name some" (Cotten 2012a: 1). A third reason included different possibilities for sexual intimacy; trying to explain one's genitals to someone with whom you may be interested in having a sexual relationship might come with a host of negative emotions. Fourth were safety and security concerns, including dealing with law enforcement, security checkpoints while traveling, and the possibility of incarceration since people are generally placed in sex-segregated jails and prisons on the basis of their genitalia alone (Jenness and Fenstermaker 2013). And finally, Cotten referred to "issues of sovereignty and quality of life," such as legal issues surrounding what is required to be able to change the sex/gender designation on a birth certificate or identity documents and the ramifications this may have on citizenship, naturalization, parental rights, enforcement of bathroom policies, nullification of marriages and all the associated rights (2012a).

While some of the reasons for genital surgery may apply equally to trans* people of all races, males of color are statistically more at risk for concerns around safety and security due to racial profiling, stop and frisk policies, and institutional racism that pervade U.S. society (Alexander 2012). Indeed, both Black trans* males I interviewed discussed at length the increased scrutiny they received from police and other security personnel. And while both of them had undergone genital surgeries, trans* males of color are also less likely to have the financial means and access to these surgeries. This is because the same institutionalized racism that places them at higher risk for violations of their safety and security also closely links race to class in our society. In these ways, race, in addition to class, is a significant part of a web of intersecting exclusions and makes a difference between trans* males' legs.

Eldercare: Caring For the Aging

While healthcare is an ongoing issue for many trans* people, as shown by the examples of James, Charlotte, Kevin, and Walks With Two Spirits, the issue is clearly complicated by ethno-racial and class dynamics here in the United States. In a similar fashion, age also creates an added dimension to these complexities.

Due to the growing numbers of older trans* people, a new set of doctors also now need training: those in **geriatric medicine**. Additionally, eldercare facilities are currently facing policy and procedural challenges around working with lesbian and gay clients due to the sex-segregation and **heteronormative** assumptions of many facilities, to which trans* people add complications. Because lesbian, gay, and trans* elders now entering later-life generally came out during a time in which being out meant losing connections to family of orientation, they are more heavily dependent on eldercare facilities than their heterosexual and cis* peers. What provisions then are trans* people making to secure later-life care in ways that allow for the smooth continuation of being seen as they wish to be seen, and what alternative resources to family of orientation support are at their disposal?

Eldercare was of considerable concern to Benji. Benji, a trans* male with mixed Asian/White parentage first introduced in

Chapter Two, moved to the United States at the age of 18 from the Philippines. Fifty-four by the time of our meeting, he considered himself very much American. I met him at his single-family home in a town near Seattle where he lived alone. He had short black hair, a mustache, and a small goatee, peppered with grey, and wore a dark colored long-sleeved shirt under a White polo with a dark green collar and stripes.

During the course of our conversation Benji spoke a bit about healthcare more broadly in ways that included issues about the possibility of moving and finding new, sympathetic doctors. He then discussed healthcare from the perspective of aging and shared how he had talked with his primary care physician about eldercare issues. Benji commented:

> My healthcare provider actually mentioned that as our group ages and we wind up being in nursing homes and things like that, how will we be taken care of? What kind of treatment will we get? Will we be respected? Will we be abused? Will there just be great insensitivity towards us and our issues? We'll be very vulnerable like everyone is in that situation. How will that impact our dignity? Being in diapers is bad enough . . . Being referred to as she?

Benji pointed out that at 54, his own age was only part of his recently growing concern about how trans* elders will be treated. He noted:

> I know you can just laugh about it, but it does frighten me. My mom just passed away a couple of years ago. At the end of her life, she wound up in a nursing home so I got to see how she was treated there. My mother was a physician so she was in the medical profession and to see that even as a physician, the kind of compromised care she got, I'm thinking what hope do I have?

It seemed a perfectly reasonable concern that if a doctor like his mother, who we might expect would benefit from mutual professional respect when it came to eldercare was treated poorly, there was little reason to believe trans* people would fare better.

Michael also expressed concerns about the treatment of trans* elders. Michael, a White trans* male, had just turned 50 a few days before I went to interview him in his home in San Francisco, California. He was dressed in a grey t-shirt and distressed black jeans. He wore his facial hair in a mustache and goatee style, his hair was greying, and he was beginning to go bald on top. He reclined on a green leather sofa in his living room for our conversation and I sat in a matching armchair and used the ottoman for my laptop and recorder.

Michael started medical transition at 37 years old, which at the time of our meeting, had included hormones, chest reconstruction, and a complete hysterectomy. He had thought off and on about genital surgery, especially since his current healthcare insurance contracted with two well-known trans* surgery specialists and covered the vast majority of surgical costs. Still, he had some concerns about surgical options and his own motivations. Interestingly, thinking about eldercare tended to contribute to contemplations about genital surgery. He noted he had heard, "horror stories about people being abused basically because their bodies are freakish to the workers who are there." This led him to wonder, "if I had lower surgery would that make it easier as I get older to do whatever needs to happen and not worry about how are people going to react to my body?" He balanced these questions with concerns about the surgical risks involved with an aging body. He also worried about changing his body based on how others might react rather than changing out of a sense of personal authenticity. He explained:

> It's like . . . and how much do I want to do stuff because of other people, and that's part of the issue. It's like . . .

and so is that safety thing? There's the how do I take care of myself, how do I make sure I am taking care of what I can't take care of myself, and those things become much more present as you get older. As I am hearing more about what's happening in our elderly communities and what's available and not available to people, and you don't have the option of going in the closet. If you've created an intersex body you are going to deal with those issues.

Michael also pointed out that these issues were becoming more pressing for him because he had no children and, "I really have nobody who is going to take care of me as I get older."

Michael did express some hope for the future of trans* eldercare. He pointed out that, "Obviously the changes that have happened for the queer community have been exponential in relationship to what's happened around race, as far as changes and how quickly they've occurred." He noted that while there are only two places in the United States he considered competent and, "geared towards the . . . [lesbian/gay] community," that he believed social change would happen even more rapidly for trans* people than had occurred for gay and lesbian people.

End-of-Life Decisions: Respecting Dignity

One final issue regarding the life course for trans* people is a question about end-of-life decisions. As previously mentioned, trans* people reaching later-life stages at this moment in history may have significant disconnection from their families of orientation, which would typically be the people who carry out any end-of-life requests.

In my own recent past I had the incredibly strange and surreal experience of attending the funeral of someone I did not, but paradoxically did, know. I had known Samantha for less than a year and only knew her as Samantha at the time of her death, but I went to the funeral of Sam. Sam/Samantha lived and identified as a cross-dresser and because I knew her through trans* community connections and only in specifically trans* spaces, my interactions were always with Samantha. At least that was the case until I went to see her on her deathbed with a friend. In a hospice room just after death, was the first and only time I had ever seen Sam. Sam's family was unaware of Samantha until she lay dying, and as friends and family came to sit with her and support each other, it seemed important to her friends to let her family know. As is common at funerals, a poster of photos from the span of Sam's life sat at the entrance to the room where the service was held. I had an odd, disconnected, outsider feeling gazing at years of a life that I intellectually understood as my friend's life, but that looked to me more like photos of my friend's fraternal twin. Sam had remained in contact with his parents and his son throughout his life, but had kept Samantha and her life separate. Thus, it was more a matter of unfamiliarity rather than ostracism or disapproval that led to a funeral for Sam without Samantha. However, more troubled and heartbreaking situations also occur.

I met Lisa, a 44-year-old, Black trans* female, in a suburban community near Miami, Florida in a neighborhood that consisted mainly of single-story apartment complexes and single-family homes. The area was a working-class neighborhood with iron fencing and metal bar window-coverings often seen in poorer urban areas. I had arrived early for our appointment, so I stood in the parking spaces in front of her complex and watched as a number of people walked or rode by on bicycles. There were several cars in sight, but not as many as might be expected from the number of apartments. It appeared that many residents took the bus that dropped off about two blocks from where I stood. I remembered that Lisa was working before our meeting. After about twenty minutes of standing there

I realized that I knew she was working because we had talked about it over the phone, which meant that her number had to be in my phone somewhere. I called and she answered, telling me she was on her way home and would be there in another 15 minutes or so.

Lisa pulled up in an older model car and hopped out wearing her work uniform of khaki pants, black shoes, polo shirt and vest in the company colors with the screen-printed logo. She apologized for being late, told me work had been a little hectic, and showed me into her one-bedroom apartment where she had been living for 6 months at the time. The apartment was sparsely furnished with all the necessities, and thankfully had air conditioning as it was somewhere around 90 degrees with high humidity. In fact, halfway through the interview Lisa realized that she had only turned on the air conditioner in the front room and the one in the bedroom worked much better, so she went and turned that one on as well.

When she discussed her family's rejection of her trans* identity, the discussion took a unique turn that had not happened in earlier interviews. Lisa told the following story:

> It's strange because just the other day, I have a Facebook friend who's a transgender. She has a friend that recently passed away. She posted a post about her friend had came to her for financial help, but she wasn't able to help the friend at the time. The friend was from Arkansas. She called her father in Arkansas and was like, "Look, I'm sick. I would like to come see the family and everything." The father declined to help her and dismissed her. Shortly after that, the young lady passed away. The family in Arkansas found her a funeral home in Dallas to take the young lady and everything, but they gave specific instructions to the funeral home that if she looked anything like a woman that she wasn't going to be taken back to Arkansas to be

buried with family. My friend went to the funeral home. She cut the young lady hair and they did different things to try to make her look male, and everything. Bought suit and tie, all male attire and everything. The family came. They were sitting in the funeral home for about 30 minutes before they decided to cremate her, be done with it and everything. They went back to Arkansas and didn't take the ashes or anything.

Unsurprisingly, thinking about the family's complete disregard for the trans* female's identity had a significant effect on Lisa and she thought long and hard about what end-of-life decisions her family might make for her. Clearly upset she said, "How can family do that? I have no doubt that if, Lord forbid, something happened to me here . . . that my family will come get me and to bury me. I don't feel that my wishes will be granted to be buried as Lisa." This event got Lisa thinking about plans for how she wished to be treated at the end of her life and got her started making decisions. She explained:

After reading that post and thinking about it and everything, I've decided that I'm personally going to go ahead and start making my arrangements to be cremated. I want my ashes to be released in the Atlantic. This is my home now. This is where I feel whole. When I be released, I want to be released as Lisa. That's who I am. I know that's going to be a hard thing for my family, but it's a decision that I've come to make.

End-of-life decisions can be difficult for anyone to make. For Lisa and many in the trans* community, the challenges can be exacerbated by the willingness of family to accept a person's transition, both in life and in death.

DISCUSSION QUESTIONS

1. Check your school or employer's website or handbook for information about the health insurance benefits and what they cover. Do they cover transition related healthcare such as hormones, chest/breast and genital surgeries? Is there a transition-related care exclusion? If transition care is covered, do they list limits on the amounts insurance will cover? Is there a lifetime maximum benefit listed?

2. Conduct an internet search using the terms "transgender elder care." What are the titles of the first five links that are listed? What is the general impression this gives you about the quality of care trans* people can expect later in life?

3. Who do you expect to take care of your end-of-life decisions and make sure your wishes are followed? How might your expectations change if your experiences with family mirrored those of James in Chapter Four?

Notes

1. Updates on the progress of NCTE's efforts can be found on their website at www.transequality.org/.

2. Mons resection removes excess skin and tissue from the mons veneris, which is the "mound" that covers the pubic bone. This is removed so as not to cover the newly formed phallus created through metoidioplasty. Urethroplasty is the lengthening of the urethra, in this case using a graft of buccal membrane from inside the mouth, through the created phallus to allow for standing urination.

3. Phalloplasty is the surgical creation of a complete penis using tissue from one of several different donor sites depending on the procedural method. The donor sites are most commonly the forearm, the inner thigh, or the lower back. Each method has pros and cons in terms of healing and outcomes and phalloplasty generally consists of several separate surgeries.

4. Clitoral release involves severing the ligament holding the clitoral/penile tissue down so it protrudes more from the body. Vaginectomy involves

removal of the vaginal canal and sewing shut the remaining opening. The scrotum, or sac that holds the testicles in males, is created by sewing together the labia majora, or "outer lips" of the female external genitalia the vulva.

5. "Obamacare" is the shorthand, colloquial name for the Affordable Care Act, passed into law in 2010 under President Barack Obama.

6. For an example of techniques, process, and outcomes, see Bettocchi Ralph, and Pryor 2005.

Epilogue

I've done my activism around bathrooms for 10 years already. I've put signs on doors. I've gone and spoken at different colleges about why they need gender-neutral bathrooms. I feel like I've fought that battle and now I get to have whichever bathroom I like. If I'm in a really unsafe environment, if I was on the road at a rest stop in some conservative part of the state, I would be really cautious. I would probably just make sure to use the men's room. Around the [more liberal area], I feel like I can kind of play with it, it's okay.

—Alex

Moving Forward

Throughout this text, care has been taken in attending to multiple and simultaneously held identities in discussing the experiences of trans* people. As noted, how a trans* person is located in relation to race and ethnicity, social class, sex, and gender makes a significant difference in both the types of experiences faced and the resources that can be drawn on to meet any challenges that arise. As trans* studies continues to grow and address new ideas and areas of trans* lives, needs, and experiences, continued attention to intersectional analysis will be imperative in accurately representing and understanding trans* people.

The Realities of Risk and Violence

When I first started formally studying trans* people in graduate school, I wrote about media and activist treatment of trans* females who were victims of homicide, focusing on the case of Ruby Ordeñana (Rodriguez). In my earlier writings, I sought to call attention to the role of sex work in the telling of these stories. Sex work was hyper-visible in media accounts in order to make the homicide unremarkable. In contrast, sex work was absent in activist accounts to make the victim appear closer to the ideal of the White, innocent woman victim for the purpose of garnering sympathy for the violence perpetrated against all gender non-conforming people. I saw a pattern in these representations in that the "web of intersecting exclusions" and specifically, race matters. For example, Lydia Sausa, JoAnne Keatley, and Don Operario (2007) pointed out that here in the United States, trans* females of color "often engage in sex work for economic survival" and "participants reported on how social networks and cultural norms, immigration issues, and experiences of racism, sexism, and transphobia influenced their decisions to enter and the risks encountered in sex work" (768).

To be clear, sex work as discussed here is not the upper end of the hierarchy as in high-end escort services or even middle class in-home independent business. When talking about trans* females of color and sex work, we are talking about the least paid, most vulnerable of the sex work population: those who walk the streets on the least desirable strolls, regularly harassed by police in each cycle of "quality of life" sweeps. In the research for this book, only two participants brought up having formerly worked in the sex work industry. Unsurprisingly one of the two was Black and Native American and the other was Native American. Both trans* females.

One of the ways of measuring violence against trans* people has been through the list of trans* people murdered, which is kept on the website for the Transgender Day of Remembrance (TDoR).[1] Of course there is generally no way to know from the index card of information provided at the TDoR gatherings around the world how many of those who died in the previous year of anti-trans* violence or prejudice were sex workers. This is not surprising given the goal of painting a picture of risk where the largest numbers of people—especially those closest to the image of the ideal victim—are in harm's way and in need of protections. This strategy of removing information about the victim's life helps avoid calling up stereotypes about deserving/ undeserving victims. In this way, the discussion of transphobic violence moves from a story about an isolated victim and incident to one about a systemic social problem. According to one scholar, this strategy is important to pushing the boundaries of empathy beyond the ideal victim (Wanzo 2009). However, a focus on putting these incidents together as instances of anti-trans* violence also risks erasing a more complex picture of multiple intersecting identities that structurally place some trans* people disproportionately at risk in a multitude of ways.

Since names and location, and pictures starting in 2008 if available, are given, it is possible to recognize the disproportionate representation of trans* females of color on the list every year. In part, the list is limited by the methods of data collection. People end up on the list because someone sent the information in, not because good records are kept by any reporting or law enforcement agency. In this sense the lists are biased such that the high number of victims reported from Brazil are partly an artifact of better reporting from Brazil than from other places in the world, but also reflect a high incidence of deaths that we would consider hate crimes.[2] Indeed, as I spoke with Maya about the differing challenges faced by trans* males and trans* females, the reality of violence for trans* females hit close to home:

> I think about it all the time when I hear stories about people that were murdered or discriminated against. I'm just tired of it. You know something? Now we've just said that . . . I tell you, no lie (reading from cell phone) "Transgender woman found shot to death at east Texas. Roommate suspects hate crime." I'm in a trans* group on Facebook. Every time I turn around, every 2 or 3 days, I see something about a transgender girl being killed. One girl, a 30-year-old transgender girl in Virginia just got shot or killed 4 or 5 days ago.

Further research revealed that both women Maya mentioned, shot and killed less than a week apart, were both trans* females of color. By including (or erasing, depending on your viewpoint) all of the deaths as anti-trans* violence, it is easy to miss the point that keeping trans* people safe is not just about creating and enforcing policies aimed at transphobia, but is also integrally related to feminist and anti-racist work.

The importance of race and sex/gender in transphobic violence is visible beyond what gets reported at TDoR. Although all trans* people risk harassment, violence, and assault, it is clear that U.S. society reserves a particularly nasty experience of risk and violence for trans* females of color specifically. Looking at the *U.S. Transgender Survey*, overall rates of unequal treatment, verbal harassment, and physical attack were higher for trans* females of color than for those who were White (James et al. 2016).

Statistics support the assertion that trans* females who canno be perceived as White by others are the most vulnerable. Trans* females of color were more likely to have engaged in sex work in the past year, including 24 percent of Black trans* females, 1 percent of Latinas, Native Americans, and Asian Americans, an

12 percent of multiracial trans* females. Participation in sex work or other underground economy (criminalized) work was highest among those who had lost a job because of their trans* identity. Loss of employment was more likely among trans* females (18 percent) than anyone else in the survey (13 percent overall) and more likely for people of color (Native American 21 percent, multiracial 18 percent, 17 percent Black). Black trans* females were far more likely to be assumed by police to be engaging in sex work at 33 percent in the last year compared to 11 percent of trans* females overall. And while 6 percent of trans* females were harassed, physically or sexually assaulted, or faced some other mistreatment from police, the rate for Native American trans* women was 20 percent, with Black (17 percent) and multiracial (16 percent) trans* females also well above average. Sex workers were also more likely to have faced other forms of violence such as intimate partner violence and sexual assault. Of those who were engaged in sex work at the time of the survey, 41 percent had been physically assaulted and 36 percent had been sexually assaulted in the last year alone (James et al. 2016).

Outside of the underground economy, trans* females of color still fared worse. In K-12 schools, verbal harassment was higher for Native American and Middle Eastern trans* people. When it came to physical assault, Native American (49 percent) and Middle Eastern (36 percent) trans* people were joined by those who identified as multiracial (31 percent) and Black (28 percent) at levels above the overall average for respondents of 24 percent. Breaking the numbers down by sex/gender identity, trans* females had the highest rates of physical attack at 38 percent. These trends continued into college and vocational schools as well. In public spaces, trans* females of color also received the worst treatment from strangers, facing higher levels of verbal harassment and physical attack. In the past year alone, 11 percent of Black and Latina trans* females who had been physically attacked were attacked with a gun (James et al. 2016). Finally, in the first 3 months of 2017, eight trans* females had already been reported murdered, seven of whom were Black and one Native American (Schmider 2017). What all of these numbers add up to is the point that the most vulnerable of the trans* community, like the most vulnerable of the feminist, gay, lesbian, bisexual and many other identity communities, are those made most vulnerable by institutional racism, sexism, and classism in the United States.

Looking Beyond Transition

The majority of trans* literature to date has focused on the social and medical transition of trans* people as well as transition's immediate after-effects. Trans* people do not stop existing as *trans* people after they transition. Even if they no longer identify as trans* they still have a history of transition to contend with. For many of the trans* people who participated in my research study, although it may have become a less challenging and less noticeable aspect of identity in daily life, there were still times and places where their trans* identity became more salient. In part this is due to what I have called the *paradox of (trans*)-identity*. Looking beyond transition then enables us to examine some of the ways that trans* identity continues to hold relevance. For example, being trans* remains relevant to interaction and to whether or not ties of kinship are maintained with families of orientation as well as families of procreation for those who created families prior to transition. Unfortunately, while visibility and acceptance for trans* people are on the rise, loss of ties to both families of orientation and families of procreation are all too common for trans* people upon disclosure of a trans* identity.

Coming out and the revelations of acknowledging a trans* identity capture the popular imagination and headlines. Reaching an understanding of the self as trans*, making the decision to transition in whatever ways feel authentic, and learning to exist differently in the world are only some of the ways in which trans* identity impacts a person's life. Continuing to explore life beyond transition provides a fruitful ground for understanding trans* people in multi-dimensional ways and for contributing to the dignity and respect trans* people receive in society.

Future Research

Future studies can expand upon this work by further exploring the informal and formal social networks trans* people create in their personal and work lives and understanding the importance of these networks to the wellbeing of trans* individuals. Alternative family formations and religious community participation were also suggested by trans* people I interviewed as areas that require further exploration. Examining trans* lives not only contributes to better understanding and hopefully better treatment, but can also inform future public policy to address trans* people's needs in response to their current social location.

A cursory look at the National Center for Transgender Equality's website[3] uncovers a host of issues of importance to trans* lives. The NCTE's list includes issues of aging, anti-violence, employment, families, health and HIV, housing and homelessness, identity documents and privacy, immigration, international human rights for trans* people, the military and veterans, non-discrimination laws, police, jails and prisons, racial and economic justice, research and data needs, travel, voting rights, and youth and students. NCTE was particularly engaged in working with the Obama administration to ensure trans* people receive adequate health care, including through the Affordable Care Act. At the time of this writing, NCTE is focusing significant efforts and resources on the removal of trans*-related healthcare exclusions by health insurance companies, clarifying what trans*-related means for healthcare, and ultimately working to ensure that transition-related care, including hormonal therapy and surgeries, are covered by medical insurance.[4]

In June of 2016, the Obama administration lifted the ban on trans* people serving openly in the military.[5] As the world's largest employer, the United States military's decision is a significant victory for trans* citizens trying to make a living as their authentic selves (Chang 2015). Concerns remain, however, about the requirement that individuals who have transitioned wait 18 months after transition to enter the military (Tobin 2016). Issues also remain about what healthcare will be covered by military insurance including hormones and surgeries.

As is common with many social movements, change is often met with resistance, and progress with backlash. In the midst of growing awareness of trans* lives and needs in the United States, there is an ongoing struggle to achieve further safeguards against state-sanctioned discrimination. Since the election of Donald Trump in November of 2016, several legislative bills have been proposed in all regions of the United States to restrict the rights of trans* people. For example, backlash "bathroom bills" were already "prefiled or introduced" in 12 states in the first month of the 2017 legislative session including in Alabama, Illinois, Kansas, Kentucky, Minnesota, Missouri, South Carolina, South Dakota, Texas, Virginia, Washington, and Wyoming (Kralik 2017).[6]

These bills are aimed at testing the judicial interpretation of **Title VII of the Civil Rights Act of 1964** and **Title IX of the Education Amendments Act of 1972**. Title VII "prohibits employment discrimination based on race, color, religion, sex and national origin" (U.S. Equal Employment Opportunity Commission n.d.a). At issue is whether or not trans* people are protected under the definition of sex discrimination. Some employers and city or county governments have specifically added "gender identity and expression"[7] to nondiscrimination policies to ensure that trans* people are protected. However, as many laws do not specify "gender identity and expression," trans* people have only been specifically included in a few areas of the United States. Because federal protection laws are difficul to change, having trans* people included within the definition of sex discrimination would provide coverage throughout the United States without any additional battles to change the legislation.

The U.S. Equal Employment Opportunity Commission (EEOC) released a statement in May of 2016 which clarified that discrimination against trans* individuals amounted to sex discrimination and was therefore covered under Title VII protections (Phillips 2016; U.S. EEOC n.d.b). In this guidance, the EEOC relied on Supreme Court decisions such as *Price Waterhouse v. Hopkins*, as well as federal court rulings (U.S. EEOC n.d.c). Still, states have continued their attempts to restrict bathroom use by trans* people in violation of this guidance.

While Title VII is specifically related to employers, Title IX "protects people from discrimination based on sex in education programs or activities that receive Federal financial assistance" (U.S. Department of Education 2015). On January 15, 2015, under the Obama administration, the Department of Education (DoED) released guidance for schools that Title IX was to be interpreted as protecting the rights of trans* students (EEOC n.d.c). The case of Gavin Grimm[8] (*Grimm v. Gloucester County School Board*), a male-identified trans* high school student seeking access to the boy's restrooms at his school, has been the focus of legal interpretation of Title IX with respect to trans* students. A federal Court of Appeals decided in favor of Grimm and the case was accepted by the Supreme Court for a hearing (EEOC n.d.c). However, the Trump administration reversed the DoED guidance provided under Obama. As a result, the Supreme Court remanded the case back to the Court of Appeals to determine whether or not Title IX protects the rights of trans* students without taking into account the interpretation provided by DoED (Balingit 2017; de Vogue, Vladeck, and Schleifer 2017). It is likely that the case will return to the Supreme Court following a new ruling by the Court of Appeals.

Continued efforts to secure basic rights and shed light on pressing issues for trans* people at all stages and in all areas of their lives requires an ongoing and active research agenda. This text serves as one such starting point and hopefully will inspire many more.

DISCUSSION QUESTIONS

1. What are some of the issues currently facing trans* people in your local community? What about in the United States as a whole? You might check transequality.org or hrc.org for ideas.
2. Brainstorm individually or in a small group ways in which you might be able to get involved helping trans* people achieve equality. What are two things you could do today to get started?

Notes

1. The International Transgender Day of Remembrance website can be found at www.transgenderdor.org.
2. The list is also limited by the term and identity of trans* itself, which is both historically and geographically located. Some places on the globe may not recognize a trans* identity *as trans* locally and thus not report the deaths of people others may wish to include.
3. The National Center for Transgender Equality website can be found at www.transequality.org/.
4. For more information about NCTE's work in this area, see www.transequality.org/issues/health-hiv.
5. In July of 2017, President Trump tweeted his intent to ban trans* people from the military again. The status of trans* service members remains to be seen.
6. For media coverage about bathroom bills see also New York Times 2017 Peters, Becker, and Davis 2017; Ura, Blanchard, and Wiseman 2017.

7. While I note in Chapter One that sex identity and gender identity are separate, the two are frequently conflated. In some ways discrimination is based on the idea that a trans* person has a different sex identity (male or female) than they were assigned at birth. However, it is also related to the gender (masculinity or femininity) the individual is performing, particularly if they are performing in a way incongruent with their birth-assigned sex. In mainstream discussions including legal and policy discussions, however, gender identity and gender expression are understood to be the categories for the protection of trans* people.

8. Not the Gavin I interviewed.

Appendix A
Research Methods

This is a qualitative study that draws upon research conducted over a period of 21 months beginning in October of 2013. I conducted semi-structured, in-depth, face-to-face interviews with thirty individuals. The participants interviewed included 14 trans* females, 15 trans* males, and 1 genderqueer identified individual. All participants were over the age of 18 years old, reported being 5 or more years into/post transition, and have had some medical modification to the sex of their bodies (hormones, chest reconstruction, metoidioplasty, phalloplasty, vaginoplasty).

I utilized a multi-method approach in recruiting participants for this study. I used four avenues to identify potential research participants. These research strategies included: 1) Attendance and participation in a conference, 2) Advertising in the conference program, 3) Contacting regional LGBTQ organizations, and 4) snowball sampling.

In August of 2013 I attended "Gender Odyssey," an annual conference for trans* people. I began recruiting participants for this study at this conference. I ran an advertisement for the study in the conference program. Information advertising this research study was also sent by participants to others in their networks whom they believed might be interested in participating. In addition to these methods, I also contacted listserves and groups local to the areas where I already planned to travel in order to meet with initial contacts from the conference.

I identified and interviewed trans* people who resided in twenty-two cities in eight states and five regions (South, Southeast, Midwest, Pacific Northwest, West Coast) of the United States, with a variety of diverse identities and experiences. Each interview was audio recorded and lasted between 75 minutes and 180 minutes. Interviews were conducted at the respondent's current residence or a family or friend's residence, except in three cases where respondents requested that we meet in a private office.[1] Interviews were digitally recorded then transcribed and coded for emerging themes.

Drawing on grounded theory, this study expands understanding about the ways in which a trans* identity continues beyond transition itself. Analyzing the narrative explanations given by the interviewees and systematically coding them for themes allowed me to identify larger patterns in the data. Because attending to themes began with the first interviews, it was also possible to adjust future interviews to better attend to emerging themes (Glaser and Strauss [1967] 2010).

I employed a grounded theory approach in order to better respond to the competing needs of the academic and trans* communities. Glaser and Strauss ([1967] 2010) argued that because grounded theory is derived from empirical research, the theory that emerges remains understandable to the community from which it is drawn. This was a particularly appropriate method, given that an important use of this data is to help trans* people understand the challenges that arise from an ongoing trans* identity and to provide a forum for helping trans* people help each other in managing these challenges. Given the dearth of information about post-transition life, this study was ideally suited to a grounded theory approach, where new discoveries could inform the theory from the outset (Glaser and Strauss [1967] 2010).

Qualitative methods were the most fruitful for gathering data about the ways in which trans* identity creates ongoing challenges throughout the life cycle. Furthermore, given the vulnerability of this population, trans* people may be reluctant to participate in research for fear of being stigmatized and out of concern for research misuse. Thus, face-to-face interaction was best suited for developing the trust required to collect the most accurate data (Glaser and Strauss [1967] 2010). For this reason, I travelled extensively throughout five regions in the United States to interview people for all thirty interviews. Consequently, I am able to illuminate the trans* life cycle and provide a nuanced analysis of the struggles of living as our authentic selves within a sociological context, and also bring together a "collected wisdom" of those who have come before to share with generations of trans* people to come.

Note

1. At the beginning of each interview, participants were given a page of open-ended demographic information questions to complete on a laptop, or I asked the questions and I recorded the respondent's answers verbatim. Each participant was then given a list of "agenda items," including the main research question and possible areas of discussion, to discuss in the order of their choosing. Participants were probed for clarification of information or expansion upon ideas in the course of the conversation. Upon completion of the demographic information, interviewees were asked to provide recorded verbal consent to participate and then were asked to begin the interview portion with a brief overview of their transition.

Appendix B
Participant Demographics

Participant Demographic Information

Name	Age	Race/Ethnicity	Income	Education	In Relationship
Alex	39	White	$70,000	MA	No
Anne	56	White	$33,000	BA	No
Benji	54	Asian/White	usually ~$85,000, training ~$30,000	MA	No
Brad	34	White	$31,000	Some College	Yes
Carlos	late forties	Latino	$68,000	3 graduate degrees	Yes
Charlotte	41	White	<$20,000	AA	No
David	49	White	"Upper Middle"	BA and professional designations	No
Donna	63	White	$24,000	Some College	Yes
Eduardo	36	Chicano	$80,000	JD	No
Eli	40	White	$18,000	AA, working on MA	No
Gavin	32	White	$75,000	PhD	Yes
Heather	52	White	$75,000	BA	Yes
James	49	White	$35,000	DMA	Yes
Jess	29	White	$10,000	BA	Yes
Kevin	33	Black	$45,000	BS	No
Leddy	45	White	$70,000	Voc. Tech. 4 years	Yes
Lisa	44	Black	$28,000	Some College	No
Magic	43	White	varies	ND (naturopathic doctor)	Yes
Maya	26	Black (Haitian)	$22,000	Some College	No
Michael	50	White	$150,000	PhD	Yes
Monique	49	Black	$36,000	BS	No
Nima	48	"Mixed"	<$15,000	Some College	No
Noah	46	White	<$20,000	BA	No
Penny	56	White	$120,000	MS	No
Red	42	White	0	AA	No
Riley	49	White	$53,000	PhD	No
Ryzha	36	Black/Native American	$35,000	Some College	No
Taye	late forties	Black	$70,000	PhD	Yes
Walks With Two Spirits	57	Native American/French	$12,000	GED	Yes
Zoe	52	White	$50,000 (with partner)	GED	Yes

Bibliography

Ackerman, Joshua M., Jenessa R. Shapiro, Steven L. Neuberg, Douglas T. Kenrick, D. Vaughn Becker, Vladas Griskevicius, Jon K. Maner, and Mark Schaller. 2006. "They All Look the Same To Me (Unless They're Angry) From Out-group Homogeneity To Out-group Heterogeneity." *Psychological Science* 17(10): 836–840.

Adkins, Lisa, and Beverly Skeggs, Eds. 2004. *Feminism After Bourdieu.* Oxford: Blackwell.

Alexander, Claire, and Caroline Knowles. 2005. *Making Race Matter: Bodies, Space, and Identity.* London: Palgrave.

Alexander, Michelle. 2012. *The New Jim Crow: Mass Incarceration in the Age of Colorblindness.* New York: The New Press.

Ali, Suki. 2003. *Mixed-Race, Post-Race: Gender, New Ethnicities and Cultural Practices.* Oxford: Berg.

Auldridge, Allison, Anne Tamar-Mattis, Sean Kennedy, Emily Ames, and Harper Jean Tobin. 2012. "Improving the Lives of Transgender Older Adults: Recommendations for Policy and Practice." Retrieved April 16, 2014 (http://transequality.org/Resources/TransAgingPolicyReportFull.pdf).

Balingit, Moriah. 2017. "Transgender Teen's Road to the Supreme Court Detours, But Story Is Not Over." *The Washington Post,* March 7. Retrieved March 18, 2017 (www.washingtonpost.com/local/education/transgender-teens-road-to-the-supreme-court-detours-but-his-story-is-not-over/2017/03/07/b8c1d010–02a0-11e7-b9fa-ed727b644a0b_story.html?utm_term=.678383fe3225).

Banks, Ingrid. 1998. *Hair Matters: Beauty, Power and Black Women's Consciousness.* New York: New York University Press.

Barnett, Bernice McNair. 1993. "Invisible Southern Black Women Leaders in the Civil Rights Movement: The Triple Constraints of Gender, Race, and Class." *Gender & Society* 7(2): 162–182.

Benokraitis, Nijole. 2015. *Marriages and Families: Changes, Choices, and Constraints*, 8th ed., New York: Pearson.

Berry, D. Channsin and Bill Duke. 2011. *Dark Girls.* USA. 71 minutes.

Bettocchi, Carlo, David J. Ralph, and John P. Pryor. 2005. "Pedicled Pubic Phalloplasty in Females With Gender Dysphoria." *BJU International* 95(1): 120–124.

Bishop, Katelynn. 2016. "Body Modification and Trans Men: The Lived Realities of Gender Transition and Partner Intimacy." *Body & Society* 22(1): 62–91.

Bolonik, Kera. 2015. "Julia Sweeney's 'SNL' backstage stories: 'You could just watch how many more Adam Sandler and David Spade and Chris Farley sketches there are, that white-male energy that I wasn't part of.'" *Salon*, May 5. Retrieved July 30, 2015 (www.salon.com/2015/05/05/ julia_sweeneys_snl_backstage_stories_you_could_just_watch_how_ many_more_adam_sandler_and_david_spade_and_chris_farley_ sketches_there_are_that_white_male_energy_that_i_wasnt_part_of/).

Bordo, Susan. 1993. *Unbearable Weight: Feminism, Western Culture, and the Body.* Berkeley, CA: University of California Press.

Bornstein, Kate. 1994. *Gender Outlaw: On Men, Women, and the Rest of Us.* New York: Routledge.

Bourdieu, Pierre. 1984. *Distinction: A Social Critique of the Judgement of Taste.* Cambridge, MA: Harvard University Press.

Bourdieu, Pierre. 1997. "The Forms of Capital," pp. 241–258 in *Education: Culture, Economy, and Society*, A.H. Haley, Hugh Lauder, Phillip Brown, and Amy Stuart Wells (Eds.). Oxford: Oxford University Press.

Boylan, Jennifer Finney. 2003. *She's Not There: A Life in Two Genders.* New York: Broadway Books.

Brigham, John C., and Paul Barkowitz. 1978. "Do 'They all look alike?' The Effect of Race, Sex, Experience, and Attitudes on the Ability to Recognize Faces1." *Journal of Applied Social Psychology* 8(4): 306–318

Brumberg, Joan Jacob. 1997. *The Body Project: An Intimate History of American Girls.* New York: Vintage Books.

Budge, Stephanie L., Jill L. Adelson, and Kimberly A.S. Howard. 2013. "Anxiety and Depression in Transgender Individuals: The Roles of Transition Status, Loss, Social Support, and Coping." *Journal of Consulting and Clinical Psychology* 81(3): 545–557.

Burke, Peter J., and Jan E. Stets. 2009. *Identity Theory.* Oxford: Oxford University Press.

Butler, Judith. 1988. "Performative Acts and Gender Constitution: An Essay in Phenomenology and Feminist Theory." *Theatre Journal* 4: 519–531. Retrieved June 15, 2011 (www.jstor.org/stable/3207893).

Butler, Judith. [1990] 2007. *Gender Trouble.* New York: Routledge.

Carmichael, Stokely and Charles Hamilton. 1967. *Black Power: The Politics of Liberation in America.* New York: Vintage.

Butler, Judith. [1993] 2011. *Bodies That Matter.* New York: Routledge.

Centers for Disease Control and Prevention. 2016. "2015 National Health Interview Survey: Sample Adult File." Retrieved April 7, 2017 (ftp:// ftp.cdc.gov/pub/Health_Statistics/NCHS/ Dataset_Documentation/ NHIS/2015/samadult_freq.pdf).

Chang, Sue. 2015. "U.S. Military Is the Largest Employer in the World." *MarketWatch,* June 17. Retrieved October 28, 2015 (www.market watch.com/story/us-military-is-the-largest-employer-in-the-world-2015–06–17).

Clare, Eli. 2009. *Exile & Pride: Disability, Queerness and Liberation.* Cambridge, MA: South End Press Classics.

Collins, Patricia Hill. 2004. *Black Sexual Politics: African Americans, Gender, and the New Racism.* New York: Routledge.

Combahee River Collective. 1978. "The Combahee River Collective Statement," pp. 362–372 in *Capitalist Patriarchy and the Case for Socialist Feminism,* Zillah Eisenstein (Ed.). New York: Monthly Review Press.

Conley, Dalton. 2008. *You May Ask Yourself: An Introduction to Thinking Like a Sociologist.* New York: Norton.

Cotten, Trystan T., Ed. 2012a. *Hung Jury: Testimonies of Genital Surgery by Transsexual Men.* Oakland, CA: Transgress Press.

Cotten, Trystan T. 2012b. *Transgender Migrations: The Bodies, Borders, and Politics of Transition.* New York: Routledge.

Crawford, Vicki L., Jacqueline Anne Rouse, and Barbara Woods, Eds. 1990. *Women in the Civil Rights Movement: Trailblazers and Torchbearers, 1941–1965*. Bloomington, IN: Indiana University Press.

Crenshaw, Kimberlé. 1989. "Demarginalizing the Intersection of Race and Sex: A Black Feminist Critique of Antidiscrimination Doctrine, Feminist Theory and Antiracist Politics." *The University of Chicago Legal Forum* 140: 139–167. Retrieved March 14, 2017 (https://philpapers.org/rec/CREDTI).

Crenshaw, Kimberlé. 1991. "Mapping the Margins: Intersectionality, Identity Politics, and Violence Against Women of Color." *Stanford Law Review* 43: 1241–1299.

de Vogue, Ariane, Steve Vladeck, and Theodore Schleifer. 2017. "Supreme Court Sends Transgender Case Back to Lower Court." *CNN*, March 6. Retrieved March 18, 2017 (www.cnn.com/2017/03/06/politics/gavin-grimm-transgender-case-supreme-court/).

Devor, Aaron H. 2004. "Witnessing and Mirroring: A Fourteen Stage Model Of Transsexual Identity Formation." *Journal Of Gay & Lesbian Psychotherapy* 8(1/2): 41–67. Retrieved October 22, 2011 (http://web.uvic.ca/~ahdevor/14StagesBLOCK.pdf).

Devor, Holly. 1997. *FTM: Female-to-Male Transsexuals in Society*. Bloomington, IN: Indiana University Press.

Diamond, Lisa M. 2008. *Sexual Fluidity: Understanding Women's Love and Desire*. Cambridge, MA: Harvard University Press.

Diamond, Lisa M., Seth T. Pardo, and Molly R. Butterworth. 2011. "Transgender Experience and Identity," pp. 629–647 in *Handbook of Identity Theory and Research*, S. Schwartz, K. Luyckx, and V. Vignoles, (Eds.). New York: Springer.

Dozier, Raine. 2005. "Beards, Breasts, and Bodies: Doing Sex in a Gendered World." *Gender & Society* 19: 297–316.

Edmonds, Alexander. 2010. *Pretty Modern: Beauty, Sex, and Plastic Surgery in Brazil*. Durham, NC: Duke University Press.

Fausto-Sterling, Anne. 2000. *Sexing the Body: Gender Politics and the Construction of Sexuality*. New York: Basic Books.

Fenstermaker, Sarah, and Candace West. 2002. *Doing Gender, Doing Difference: Inequality, Power, and Institutional Change*. New York: Routledge, Psychology Press.

Flores, Andrew R., Taylor N.T. Brown, and Andrew S. Park. 2016. *Public Support for Transgender Rights: A Global Survey*. Los Angeles, CA: The Williams Institute. Retrieved March 9, 2017 (http://williamsinstitute. law.ucla.edu/wpcontent/uploads/International).

Flores, Andrew R., Jody L. Herman, Gary J. Gates, and Taylor N. T. Brown. 2016. *How Many Adults Identify As Transgender in the United States?* Los Angeles, CA: The Williams Institute.

Foucault, Michel. 1995. *Discipline and Punish: The Birth of the Prison* 2nd ed. New York: Vintage.

Frankenberg, Ruth. 1993. *White Women, Race Matters: The Social Construction of Whiteness*. Minneapolis, MN: University of Minnesota Press.

Fryar C.D., Q. Gu, C.L. Ogden, and K.M. Flegal. 2016. Anthropometric Reference Data for Children and Adults: United States, 2011–2014. National Center for Health Statistics. Vital Health Stat 3(39). Retrieved November 4, 2016 (www.cdc.gov/nchs/data/series/sr_03/sr03_039. pdf).

Gamson, Joshua. 1998. *Freaks Talk Back: Tabloid Talk Shows and Sexual Nonconformity*. Chicago, IL: University of Chicago Press.

Gee, Gilbert C., Katrina M. Walsemann, and Elizabeth Brondolo. 2012. "A Life Course Perspective On How Racism May Be Related to Health Inequities." *American Journal of Public Health* 102(5): 967–974.

Gender Odyssey. 2011. *Gender Odyssey: A National Conference Focused on the Thoughtful Exploration of Gender—Open to All*. Conference program for August 5–7, 2011, Seattle, WA.

Glaser, Barney G., and Anselm L. Strauss. [1967] 2010. *The Discovery of Grounded Theory: Strategies for Qualitative Research*. New Brunswick, NJ: Aldine Transaction.

Goffman, Erving. [1963] 1986. *Stigma: Notes on the Management of Spoiled Identity*. New York: Simon and Schuster.

Gonsiorek, J.C. 1988. Mental Health Issues of Gay and Lesbian Adolescents. *Journal of Adolescent Health Care* 9: 114–122.

Greenwald, Anthony G., and Mahzarin R. Banaji. 1995. "Implicit Social Cognition: Attitudes, Self-esteem, and Stereotypes." *Psychological Review* 102(1): 4.

Greenwald, Anthony G., Brian A. Nosek, and Mahzarin R. Banaji. 2003. "Understanding and Using the Implicit Association Test:

I. An Improved Scoring Algorithm." *Journal of Personality and Social Psychology* 85(2): 197.

Halberstam, Judith. 1998. "Transgender Butch: Butch/FTM Border Wars and the Masculine Continuum." *GLQ: A Journal of Lesbian and Gay Studies* 4(2): 287–310.

Herring, Cedric, Verna Keith, and Hayward Derrick Horton. 2004. *Skin Deep: How Race and Complexion Matter in the "Color-blind" Era.* Champaign, IL: University of Illinois Press.

Hickey, Darby. 2008. "Policing Gender and Sexuality: Transgender Sex Workers, HIV, and Justice." Retrieved May 12, 2010 (www.tpan.com/positivelyaware/2008/08_04/policing_gender_sexuality.html).

Hochschild, Jennifer L., and Vesla Weaver. 2007. "The Skin Color Paradox and the American Racial Order." *Social Forces* 86(2): 643–670.

hooks, bell. 1984. *Feminist Theory: From Margin to Center.* Boston, MA: South End Press.

Hull, Gloria T., Patricia Bell-Scott, and Barbara Smith. 1982. *All the Women are White, All the Blacks are Men, But Some of Us are Brave: Black Women's Studies.* Old Westbury, NY: Feminist Press.

Human Rights Campaign. 2004. "Transgender Issues in the Workplace: A Tool For Managers." Washington, DC: Human Rights Campaign. Retrieved October 8, 2015 (www.srsglobe.org/Images/HRC%20 Transgender%20tools%20for%20manager.pdf).

Hunter, Margaret. 2007. "The Persistent Problem of Colorism: Skin Tone, Status, and Inequality." *Sociology Compass* 1(1): 237–254.

International Transgender Day of Remembrance Website. www.transgenderd or.org.

James, Sandy E., Jody L. Herman, Susan Rankin, Mara Keisling, Lisa Mottet, and Ma'ayan Anafi. 2016. *The Report of the 2015 U.S. Transgender Survey.* Washington, DC: National Center for Transgender Equality.

Janken, Kenneth R. n.d. "The Civil Rights Movement: 1919–1960s." Freedom's Story, TeacherServe. National Humanities Center. Retrieved March 14, 2017 (http://nationalhumanitiescenter.org/tserve/freedom/ 1917beyond/essays/crm.htm).

Jenness, Valerie, and Sarah Fenstermaker. 2013. "Agnes Goes to Prison: Gender Authenticity, Transgender Inmates in Prisons for Men, and Pursuit of 'The Real Deal.'" *Gender & Society* 28: 5–31.

Kessler, Suzanne J., and Wendy McKenna. 1978. *Gender: An Ethnomethodological Approach*. Chicago, IL: University of Chicago Press.

Kralik, Joellen. 2017. "'Bathroom Bill' Legislative Tracking." *National Conference of State Legislatures*, February 1. Retrieved February 1, 2017 (www.ncsl.org/research/education/-bathroom-bill-legislative-tracking 635951130.aspx).

Kulick, Don. 1998. *Travesti: Sex, Gender, and Culture Among Brazilian Transgendered Prostitutes*. Chicago, IL: University of Chicago Press.

Lareau, Annette. 2002. "Invisible Inequality: Social Class and Childrearing in Black Families and White Families." *American Sociological Review* 67(5): 747–776.

Lee, Henry K. 2006. "Three Sentenced to Prison in Araujo Slaying." *San Francisco Chronicle*, January 27. Retrieved October 16, 2015 (www.sfgate.com/news/article/Three-sentenced-to-prison-in-Araujo-slaying-2542846.php).

Livingston, Jennie. 1991. *Paris is Burning*. USA. 78 minutes.

Lorber, Judith. 1994. *Paradoxes of Gender*. New Haven, CT: Yale University Press.

Lucal, Betsy. 1999. "What it Means to be Gendered Me: Life on the Boundaries of a Dichotomous Gender System." *Gender & Society* 13(6): 781–797.

Mantilla, Karla, and Alden Waitt, Eds. 2011. *Race and Transgender Studies: A Special Issue. Feminist Studies* 37(2). College Park, MD: Feminist Studies, Inc.

McCall, George J. 2003. "The Me and the Not-Me: Positive and Negative Poles of Identity," pp. 11–25 in *Advances in Identity Theory and Research*, Peter J. Burke, Timothy J. Owens, Richard T. Serpe, and Peggy A. Thoits (Eds.). New York: Kluwer/Plenum.

Maccio, Elaine M., and Kristin M. Ferguson. 2016. "Services to LGBTQ Runaway and Homeless Youth: Gaps and Recommendations." *Children and Youth Services Review* 63: 47–57.

McIntosh, Peggy. 1998. "White Privilege," pp. 94–105 in *Race, Class and Gender: An Anthology*, Margaret Anderson and Patricia Hill Collins (Eds.) 2nd ed. Belmont, CA: Wadsworth Publishing Company.

McKinney, Karyn D. 2005. *Being White: Stories of Race and Racism*. New York: Routledge.

Mennicke, Annelise, and Andrew Cutler-Seeber. 2016. "Incorporating Inclusivity: How Organizations Can Improve the Workplace Experiences of Trans* People Across the Trans* Spectrum" in *Sexual Orientation and Transgender Issues in Organizations—Global Perspectives on LGBT Workforce Diversity.* Thomas Köllen (Ed.). New York: Springer.

Meyerowitz, Joanne. 2002. *How Sex Changed: A History of Transsexuality in the United States.* Cambridge, MA: Harvard University Press.

Miniño Arialdi M., Jiaquan Xu, Kenneth D. Kochanek, and Betzaida Tejada-Vera. 2009. "Death in the United States, 2007." *National Center for Health Statistics Data Brief No. 26.* Retrieved March 17, 2017 (www.cdc.gov/nchs/data/databriefs/db26.pdf).

Mock, Janet. 2014. *Redefining Realness: My path to Womanhood, Identity, Love & So Much More.* New York: Simon and Schuster.

Namaste, Viviane K. 2000. *Invisible Lives: The Erasure of Transsexual and Transgendered People.* Chicago, IL: University of Chicago Press.

Narinesingh, Rajée Rajindra. 2012. *Beyond Face Value: A Journey to True Beauty, A Memoir.* IUniverse.

Nayak, Anoop. 1997. "Tales From the Darkside: Negotiating Whiteness in School Arenas." *International Studies in Sociology of Education* 7(1): 57–80.

New York Times. 2017. "Understanding Transgender Access Laws." *The New York Times,* February 24. Retrieved March 19, 2017 (www.nytimes.com/2017/02/24/us/transgender-bathroom-law.html).

Noble, Denise. 2005. "Remembering Bodies, Healing Histories: The Emotional Politics of Everyday Freedom," in *Making Race Matter: Bodies, Space, and Identity,* Claire Alexander and Caroline Knowles (Eds.). London: Palgrave.

Peters, Jeremy W., Jo Becker, and Julie Hirschfeld Davis. 2017. "Trump Rescinds Rules on Bathrooms for Transgender Students." *The New York Times,* February 22. Retrieved March 19, 2017 (www.nytimes.com/2017/02/22/us/politics/devos-sessions-transgender-students-rights.html).

Phillips, Michelle E. 2016. "EEOC Stresses Title VII Bars Discrimination Against Transgender Workers, Including Regarding Bathroom Access." *Jackson Lewis,* May 4. Retrieved March 18, 2017 (www.jacksonlewis

com/publication/eeoc-stresses-title-vii-bars-discrimination-against-transgender-workers-including-regarding-bathroom-access).Pitts, Victoria. 2003. *In the Flesh: The Cultural Politics of Body Modification*. London: Palgrave Macmillan.

Pratt, Minnie Bruce. 1984. "Identity: Skin, Blood, Heart," pp. 11–63 in *Yours in Struggle: Three Feminist Perspectives on Anti-Semitism and Racism*, Elly Bulkin, Minnie Bruce Pratt, and Barbara Smith (Eds.). Brooklyn, NY: Long Haul Press.

Prosser, Jay. 1998. *Second Skins: The Body Narratives of Transsexuality*. New York: Columbia University Press.

Psychology Today. 2017. "Gender Dysphoria." *Psychology Today* online, March 30. Retrieved April 7, 2017 (www.psychologytoday.com/conditions/gender-dysphoria).

Rahilly, Elizabeth P. 2015. "The Gender Binary Meets the Gender-Variant Child Parents' Negotiations with Childhood Gender Variance." *Gender & Society* 29(3): 338–361.

Ramirez, Tanisha Love. 2016. "Why People Are Using The Term 'Latinx'." *Huffington Post*, July 5. Retrieved March 31, 2017 (www.huffingtonpost.com/entry/why-people-are-using-the-term-latinx_us_57753328e4b0cc0fa136a159).

Reck, Jen. 2009. "Homeless Gay and Transgender Youth of Color in San Francisco: 'No One Likes Street Kids'—Even in the Castro." *Journal of LGBT Youth* 6(2–3): 223–242.

Robnett, Belinda. 1997. *How Long? How Long?: African-American Women in the Struggle for Civil Rights*. Oxford: Oxford University Press.

Roen, Katrina. 2002. "Either/Or and Both/Neither: Discursive Tensions in Transgender Politics." *Signs*. 27: 501–522.

Roser, Max. 2016. "Human Height." Retrieved November 4, 2016 (https://ourworldindata.org/human-height/).

Rubin, Henry. 2003. *Self-Made Men: Identity and Embodiment Among Transsexual Men*. Nashville, TN: Vanderbilt University Press.

Rupp, Leila J. 2012. "Sexual Fluidity 'Before Sex'." *Signs* 37(4): 849–56.

Sausa, Lydia A., JoAnne Keatley, and Don Operario. 2007. "Perceived Risks and Benefits of Sex Work Among Transgender Women of Color in San Francisco." *Archives of Sexual Behavior* 36(6): 768–777.

Savin-Williams, Ritch C. 1994. "Verbal and Physical Abuse as Stressors in the Lives of Lesbian, Gay Male, and Bisexual Youths: Associations With School Problems, Running Away, Substance Abuse, Prostitution, and Suicide." *Journal of Consulting and Clinical Psychology* 62(2): 261.

Schilt, Kristen. 2010. *Just One of the Guys? Transgender Men and the Persistence of Gender Inequality*. Chicago, IL: University of Chicago Press.

Schmider, Alex. 2017. "GLAAD Calls For Increased and Accurate Media Coverage of Transgender Murders." *GLAAD.org*, February 22, updated regularly. Retrieved March 31, 2017 (www.glaad.org/blog/glaad-calls-increased-and-accurate-media-coverage-transgender-murders).

Seeber, Andrew R. 2013. "Becoming Some*Body*: Motivations for Changing Sex Characteristics and Transpeople's Understandings of Their Behaviors in Social Context." Masters thesis submitted to The University of California, Santa Barbara, CA.

Segrest, Mab. 1994. *Memoir of a Race Traitor*. Boston, MA: South End Press.

Serano, Julia. 2007. *Whipping Girl: A Transsexual Woman on Sexism and the Scapegoating of Femininity*. Emeryville, CA: Seal Press.

Shapiro, Judith. 1991. "Transsexualism: Reflections on the Persistence of Gender Ambiguity and the Mutability of Sex," pp. 248–279 in *Body Guards: The Cultural Politics of Gender* Julia Epstein and Kristina Straub (Eds.). New York: Routledge.

Shilling, Chris. 1991. "Educating the Body: Physical Capital and the Production of Social Inequalities." *Sociology* 25(4): 653–672.

Shilling, Chris. 2003. *The Body and Social Theory*. London: SAGE Publications.

Smedley, Brian D. 2012. "The Lived Experience of Race and Its Health Consequences." *American Journal of Public Health* 102(5): 933–935.

Smith, Steven M., Veronica Stinson, and Matthew A. Prosser. 2004. "Do They All Look Alike? An Exploration of Decision-Making Strategies in Cross-Race Facial Identifications." *Canadian Journal of Behavioural Science/Revue Canadienne des Sciences du Comportement* 36(2): 146.

Snow, David A., and Sarah Anne Soule. 2010. *A Primer on Social Movements* New York: W.W. Norton.

Snyder, T.D., Cristobal de Brey, and Sally A. Dillow. 2016. *Digest of Education Statistics 2015* (NCES 2016–014). National Center for Education Statistics, Institute of Education Sciences. Washington

DC: U.S. Department of Education. Retrieved March 20, 2017 (https://nces.ed.gov/pubs2016/2016014_1.pdf).

Stryker, Susan. 2008. *Transgender History*. Berkeley, CA: Seal Press.

Stryker, Susan, and Aren Z. Aizura, Eds. 2013. *The Transgender Studies Reader 2*. New York: Routledge.

Stryker, Susan, and Stephen Whittle, Eds. 2006. *The Transgender Studies Reader*. New York: Routledge.

Supreme Court of the United States. 2015. *Obergefell et al. v. Hodges*. Retrieved October 26, 2015 (www.supremecourt.gov/opinions/14pdf/14-556_3204.pdf).

Thomas, Stephen B., Sandra Crouse Quinn, James Butler, Craig S. Fryer, and Mary A. Garza. 2011. "Toward a Fourth Generation of Disparities Research to Achieve Health Equity." *Annual Review of Public Health* 32: 399–416.

Tobin, Harper Jean. 2016. "Pentagon Lifts Transgender Military Service Ban." *National Center for Transgender Equality*, June 30. Retrieved February 1, 2017 (www.transequality.org/blog/pentagon-lifts-transgender-military-service-ban).

Ture, Kwame, and Charles V. Hamilton. 1992. *Black Power: The Politics of Liberation*. New York: Vintage.

Twine, France Winddance. 1996. "Brown Skinned White Girls: Class, Culture and the Construction of White Identity in Suburban Communities." *Gender, Place and Culture: a Journal of Feminist Geography* 3(2): 205–224.

Twine, France Winddance. 2010. *A White Side of Black Britain: Interracial Intimacy and Racial Literacy*. Durham, NC: Duke University Press.

Twine, France Winddance, and Charles Gallagher. 2008. "The Future of Whiteness: A Map of the 'Third Wave.'" *Ethnic and Racial Studies* 31(1): 4–24.

Twine, France Winddance, and Amy C. Steinbugler. 2006. "The Gap Between Whites and Whiteness: Interracial Intimacy and Racial Literacy." *Du Bois Review* 3(2): 341–363.

Ura, Alexa, Bobby Blanchard, and Todd Wiseman. 2017. "Following North Carolina's Example, Texas Republicans Unveil 'Bathroom Bill.'" *The Washington Post*, January 5. Retrieved March 19, 2017 (www.washingtonpost.com/news/post-nation/wp/2017/01/05/following-north-carolinas-example-texas-republicans-unveil-bathroom-bill/?utm_term=.28c475549757).

U.S. Bureau of the Census. 2015. "Educational Attainment in the United States: 2015." Retrieved March 20, 2017 (www.census.gov/data/tables/2015/demo/education-attainment/p20–578.html).

U.S. Department of Education. 2015. "Title IX and Sex Discrimination." Retrieved March 18, 2017 (www2.ed.gov/about/offices/list/ocr/docs/tix_dis.html).

U.S. Equal Employment Opportunity Commission. n.d.a. "Title VII of the Civil Rights Act of 1964." Retrieved March 18, 2017 (www.eeoc.gov/laws/statutes/titlevii.cfm).

U.S. Equal Employment Opportunity Commission. n.d.b. "Fact Sheet: Bathroom Access Rights for Transgender Employees Under Title VII of the Civil Rights Act of 1964." Retrieved March 18, 2017 (www.eeoc.gov/eeoc/publications/fs-bathroom-access-transgender.cfm).

U.S. Equal Employment Opportunity Commission. n.d.c. "Examples of Court Decisions Supporting Coverage of LGBT-Related Discrimination Under Title VII." Retrieved March 18, 2017 (www.eeoc.gov/eeoc/newsroom/wysk/lgbt_examples_decisions.cfm).

Valentine, David. 2007. *Imagining Transgender: An Ethnography of a Category.* Durham, NC: Duke University Press.

Valerio, Max Wolf. 2006. *The Testosterone Files: My Hormonal and Social Transformation From Female to Male.* Berkeley, CA: Seal Press.

Vilmur, Jules. 2014. *The Complicated Geography of Alice.* CreateSpace Independent Publishing Platform.

Wanzo, Rebecca. 2009. *The Suffering Will Not Be Televised: African American Women and Sentimental Political Storytelling.* Albany, NY: State University of New York Press.

Ward, Jane. 2010. "Gender Labor: Transmen, Femmes, and Collective Work of Transgression." *Sexualities* 13: 236–254.

Weiss, Jillian T. 2007. *Transgender Workplace Diversity.* Createspace Independent Publishing Platform.

West, Candace, and Don H. Zimmerman. 1987. "Doing Gender." *Gender & Society* 1: 125–151. Retrieved October 28, 2009 (http://gas.sagepub.com).

Weston, Kath. 1991. *Families We Choose: Lesbians, Gays, Kinship.* New York: Columbia University Press.

Williams, Christine L. 1995. *Still a Man's World: Men Who Do Women's Work.* Berkeley, CA: University of California Press.

The World Professional Association for Transgender Health. 2012. *Standards of Care for the Health of Transsexual, Transgender, and Gender-Nonconforming People.* Retrieved April 17, 2014 (www.wpath.org/site_page.cfm?pk_association_webpage_menu=1351&pk_association_web page=3926).

Yavorsky, Jill E. 2016. "Cisgendered Organizations: Trans Women and Inequality in the Workplace." *Sociological Forum*m, 31(4): 948–969.

Glossary and Index

androgens a class of hormones generally called sex hormones found in higher concentrations in males than females and responsible for male sexual/reproductive development in addition to levels of sexual desire in both males and females. The most frequently discussed hormone within this class is testosterone: 43, 47–48

androgynous somewhere in between female and male, feminine and masculine in appearance: 2, 59–61, 72

authenticity 19, 66–68, 148

"bathroom bills" 155, 162–163

behavior identity the internal sense of self as preferring behaviors such as style, dress, and activities that are coded as femininity and masculinity or some combination thereof: 17 see also *gender identity*

body identity the internal sense of the body one should have being female, male, or intersex: 17 see also *sex identity*

Bornstein, Kate 5

Bourdieu, Pierre 31–34

Boylan, Jennifer Finney 16

Butler, Judith 5, 12, 14, 16, 23, 33–34, 62

chest binding a process of binding the breasts down to flatten out the appearance of the chest making it more likely to be perceived as male. There are a variety of techniques including the use of Ace bandages, tight sport bras, layered sport bras, and compression shirts or vests: 27

chest reconstruction surgical procedures designed to create a male-appearing chest, not simply the removal of breast tissue. Generally includes the reshaping of nipple and areola tissue to create smaller, male-looking nipples: 49, 64, 70, 72, 126, 134, 164

cis* short for both cisgender and cissexual, is an umbrella term for those who identify with the sex and gender assigned to them at birth: 6, 15, 35, 40, 63, 97–98, 105

cisgender term for those who identify with the gender (femininity or masculinity) generally associated with the sex they were assigned at birth: 6, 19, 109

cissexual people who identify with the sex (female or male) they were assigned at birth: 6, 19

Civil Rights Era also called the African American Civil Rights Movement or the Civil Rights Movement, refers to the social movement to end racial segregation and discrimination in the United States. While often referring to the period of 1954–1968, civil rights activism began by some accounts as early as 1919: 8

class also called socioeconomic status or social class, it is a measure of an individual's status and position within the social hierarchy. Sociologists identify one's status based upon some combination of income, wealth, education, and occupational prestige: 2, 6–9; and segregation 24; and perpetrators 54; and hierarchies 68–72, 82; and employment 122; and housing 125–128; and healthcare 136–141, 143–146

Collins, Patricia Hill 9, 35

Combahee River Collective a Black feminist lesbian organization in the 1970s and 80s, influential in pointing out that the predominantly White mainstream feminist movement did not address the needs of Black and/or lesbian feminists. The collective was important in bringing forth discussion about the need for intersectionally aware activism: 8

coming out the process of revealing one's minority status in sex, gender, or sexuality. Through this process one may, for example, tell friends, family, and others that one is gay, lesbian, or trans*. Coming out as a process is required because society generally assumes one is heterosexual and cis* until one discloses otherwise. Thus the process is an ongoing one where an individual may come out to new people and in new situations throughout their lives: 86–87, 115, 119, 160

conjugal families are the families people create by forming partnerships such as spousal relationships, and which also include the children of that partnership: 87 see also *families of procreation*

crossing living as visually sex and gender incongruent, meaning female and masculine or male and feminine, or living as openly transsexual, rather than attempting to blend in with cis* males and females: 63

dating 94–95; approaches to disclosure 95–97, 99–100; and challenges of 97–99

Diagnostic and Statistical Manual of Mental Disorders currently in its fifth edition (DSM-5), the manual used by clinicians such as psychologists and psychiatrists to diagnose mental illness: 82–83

Doing Gender sociological approach to gender that suggests gender is behavior we perform at all times and expect of others on the basis of the sex category we assume them to be. For example, those we view as female we expect to behave in a feminine fashion with respect to clothing, speech, walk, etc. We are expected to engage in all of our social roles according to a particular gendered version. Thus we are not just for example teachers, but feminine teachers if we are viewed as female, and masculine teachers if we are viewed as male: 12–14, 62

DuBois, W.E.B. 8

eldercare 146–149

embodied capital forms of power the body can provide an individual: 12, 24, 31–34; and inclusion in cis* male networks 35; and male privilege 36–37; and authenticity 37–39; and "passing" 39–43; and cross-racial identification 42, 47, 50; and age at transition 43–47; and transition direction 47–50; power of 50–55 see also *gender congruence capital and sex category capital*

ethnic capital respect and esteem (power) that accrue from the display of ethnic cultural capital such as knowledge of heritage cooking or participation in hair care regimens associated with Black identit: 32–34

estrogens a class of hormones generally called sex hormones found in higher concentrations in females than males and responsible for female sexual/reproductive development. The most commonly discussed within the class of hormones is estrogen: 43, 47–48

family of procreation considered by some an outdated term, generally refers to the family created through the joining of two adults in marriage or partnership and any children that are raised by the couple: 87, 93–94 see also *conjugal families*

family of origin or orientation family an individual is raised by—biological, step, or adoptive parents and any siblings: 86

Fausto-Sterling, Anne 5, 12, 19

FTM female-to-male transsexual. Someone assigned female at birth who transitions to identifying/living as male: 63, 70, 72

gender clusters of behaviors collectively known as feminine or masculine that individuals perform and are expected to perform on the basis of their sex category. Thus female are expected to dress, walk, talk, and generally behave in feminine fashion while males are expected to do the sam in masculine fashion: 6, 11–18; theory 11–16; as behavior (bodies/behavior) 14; as separate from bodies 16; the binary 17–18

gender congruence capital/embodied capital of gender congruence power, respect, esteem, or presumption of cultural competence that accrues for those whose gender performance (femininity or masculinity) "matches" or is congruent with societal expectations on the basis of their perceived sex category. This includes females who perform mainstream expectations of femininity and males who perform hegemonic masculinity: 25, 33–39

gender dysphoria "(formerly Gender Identity Disorder) is defined by strong, persistent feelings of identification with the opposite gender and discomfort with one's own assigned sex that results in significant distress or impairment. People with gender dysphoria desire to live as members of the opposite sex and often dress and use mannerisms associated with the other gender. For instance, a person identified as a boy may feel and act like a girl. This incongruence causes significant distress, and this distress is not limited to a desire to simply be of the other gender, but may include a desire to be of an alternative gender" (Psychology Today 2017). Note that the definition conflates gender (behavior) with desires about a particular type of body (sex): 82

gender identity one's internal sense of self as feminine, masculine, some combination of both or neither. An individual's gender identity may or may not "match" with one's sense of sex identity (female or male) in the way expected by society meaning female + feminine or male + masculine: 16–18 see also *behavior identity*

gender non-binary performing a version of gender that is neither (entirely) feminine nor masculine, regardless of sex category. For example, female and both/neither masculine and feminine: 25 see also *third gender, gender non-conforming, genderqueer*

gender non-conforming performing a version of gender that is incongruent with expectations based on one's assigned sex. For example, female and masculine or male and feminine: ix, 7, 37–38, 67, 70–71, 156 see also *third gender, gender non-binary, genderqueer*

genderqueer sometimes used to refer to performing a combination of femininity and masculinity. Also sometimes used to mean gender incongruent—masculine female or feminine male—or as a political identity to acknowledge that more than two sex/gender combinations are possible: 17, 37–38, 58, 65, 68 see also *third gender, gender non-binary, gender non-conforming*

geriatric medicine medical specialty dealing with health care of the elderly: 146

glass ceiling concept explaining the barriers to achievement and promotion in the world of employment where females (and minorities) are prevented from progressing beyond: 123

glass escalator concept explaining how those viewed as male working in jobs that are female-typed experience rapid advancement into upper management and administrative positions beyond their female peers: 123

Goffman, Erving 57–58

healthcare 131–134; accessibility and social class 134–140; accessibility and racism 140–141; insurance coverage 131–132, 161–162; insurance coverage and sex coding 141–142; exclusions and intersectionality 142–146

heteronormativity/heteronormative societal belief that female + feminine and male + masculine are the only possible combinations of bodies and behaviors, that heterosexuality is the only or normal sexual orientation, and that female + feminine people should only be married to or have sexual relationships with "opposite" male + masculine people. Appearing heteronormative is to look like one fits within the societal expectations that one is either female + feminine or male + masculine and engages only in "opposite"-sex romantic and sexual relationships: 85, 146

for trans* people if their trans* identity is or becomes known: xi, 6, 51–52, 138, 160

pass/passing born in the United States of a racist history, initially used to refer to a person able to be viewed by others as white without having all-white ancestry. In the context of trans* people, passing is used to refer to people who are able to be viewed by others as a sex category other than the one they were assigned at birth. For example, someone who was assigned female at birth, but is now viewed as male by others would be said to be passing: 27; and embodied capital 31, 34–35, 38–39, 42; and hierarchies 58–59, 61–63, 65–66, 70, 81

performativity an approach to gender from the poststructuralist/queer theory perspective that views gender as an identity we perform within the constraints of our society's norms about appropriate behavior for females and males: 12, 34, 62

phalloplasty a set of surgical procedures sometimes used for female-to-male trans* people where a phallus (penis) is constructed using tissue from elsewhere on the individual's body, usually the forearm, abdomen, or inner thigh, and grafted onto the genital region. May also include the construction of a scrotum from the labia majora and the insertion of testicular prostheses as well as the re-routing of the urethra through the newly created phallus for standing urination: 70, 134–135, 143–144

population estimate ix, 4

poststructuralism/poststructuralist a movement in philosophy and literary criticism defining itself in opposition to structuralism. Often traced to Jacques Derrida, Michel Foucault, and Roland Barthes in 1960s France, the movement is defined by ideas such as that there is no authoritative subject, but rather innumerable subject positions providing conflicting interpretation. From this perspective there is no objective truth, but rather "knowledge claims": 12–16, 23, 62

pumping the process of injecting industrial grade silicone into the body (generally the buttocks, hips, thighs, breasts, and face) to create a more female appearance. Sometimes used by those transitioning from male to female: 1–4, 62, 143

queer considered by many of older generations to be a derogatory term based on its usage in the mid-19th century United States as a slur against gay and lesbian people. The term was reclaimed by younger gay, lesbian, and other non-heteronormative people in the early 1990s as a means of political and sexual self-identity and pride: 55, 63, 91, 101, 117, 149

queer theory a field of poststructuralist theory that focuses on queer readings of texts and theorizing "queerness." Queer theory deconstructs the idea of stable sex, gender, and sexuality: 12–16, 23, 62

race a system of classifying humans into groups according to physical traits such as skin color, hair texture, and ancestry. While presumed by many to be biological, race is a socially created hierarchy used to justify unequal treatment and distribution of resources within a society: 2–3; and critical race studies 7–11; and embodied capital 31–32; and criminalization 54–55; and privilege 72–82; and employment 118–119, 128; and healthcare 141, 143–146; and violence 156–160; and protections 162

real life test/real life experience the 12-month period of time trans* people are expected to live in their preferred sex/gender as a prerequisite for hormones or surgery as outlined in the Standards of Care. Not all specialists require the real-life test before prescribing hormones, but it is generally required prior to surgery: 122

Schilt, Kristen 29, 35, 47

secondary sex characteristics 14, 21–22, 25

Second Wave Feminism period of feminist activity and thought beginning in the United States in the early 1960s and lasting until the 1980s. Also referred to as the Women's Movement: 8

sex biological aspects of being female, male, or intersex including genitalia, reproductive organs, chromosomes, hormones, and secondary sex characteristics such as breasts, facial hair, and overall body shape and size: 6–7; as body (bodies/behaviors) 14; as separate from behaviors 16; the binary 17–18

sex category identification as female, male, or intersex—attributed/assumed by others in daily life generally on the basis of secondary sex characteristics since chromosomes, hormones, and genitalia are not usually available for use in categorization; and passing 39–43; and age at transition 44–47; and transition direction 47–50; and hierarchies 66–71; and sexuality 104

sex category capital/embodied capital of sex category respect, esteem, power that accrues from the individual's ability to be perceived as *either* female or male by others. If an individual cannot be easily identified as one of these two categories by others, they face significant social disadvantages: 34; and passing 39–43; and transition 44–50; and power 50–54; and hierarchies 69; and employment 122

sex identity one's internal sense of the body they should possess, whether female, male, intersex, or some other option: 16–18

sexual fluidity the idea that the category of people (female, male, etc.) one is sexually attracted to and desires changes over the course of one's life: 105

sexual orientation 104; changes through transition 104–107

Shilling, Chris 16, 34

socioeconomic status also called social class or class, it is a measure of an individual's status and position within the social hierarchy. Sociologists identify one's status based upon some combination of income, wealth, education, and occupational prestige: 7, 125–127

sociological interactional/accountability a strain of sociological thought based in *symbolic interactionism*, which focuses on the interactions between individuals and groups as well as the expectations individuals and groups have for each other that guide their interactions: 12–16

Standards of Care (SoC) the *Standards of Care for the Health of Transsexual, Transgender, and Gender-Nonconforming People* is a publication of guidelines for health professionals on how best to treat patients presenting for treatment of gender dysphoria. The publication is updated periodically by the World Professional Association for Transgender Health (WPATH): 44

status checks moments or processes in which a variety of one's identities may be shared without one's involvement. For example, in the process of checking professional employment references, a potential employer may learn of one's status as trans* (or as a racial/ethnic minority) from a professional reference from previous employment: 117–118, 128

structural racism (also called institutional racism) refers to routine institutional practices that may appear neutral, but are designed to and/or have the effect of reproducing White privilege and perpetuating racial or ethnic inequality. The concept was developed by intellectuals and activists in the Black Power Movement and moved beyond the pre-Civil Rights concept of prejudice, which focused on the attitudes of individuals and did not account for routine institutional practices (see *Black Power: The Politics of Liberation in America* by Stokely Carmichael and Charles Hamilton 1967, republished in 1992 as Kwame Ture and Charles V. Hamilton): 11, 128

Stryker, Susan 5, 18–19, 59–60, 86

testosterone primary hormone in the class of hormones called androgens. Responsible for the sexual/reproductive development in individuals assigned male at birth. When used by those assigned female at birth, causes changes such as the lowering of the voice, growth of facial and body hair, thinning of hair on the head, redistribution of body fat, etc: 25–27, 47, 50, 64, 116, 135

Title VII of the Civil Rights Act of 1964 legal statute that prohibits employment discrimination based on race, color, religion, sex and national origin: 162–163

Title IX of the Education Amendments Act of 1972 legal statute that protects people from discrimination based on sex in education programs or activities that receive Federal financial assistance: 162–163

trans* an umbrella term for a variety of sex and gender non-conforming people including those who may identify as transsexual, transgender, non-binary, gender non-conforming, gender variant, genderqueer, gender fluid, cross-dresser, etc: ix; and scholarship and theory 5–7

trans*-er than thou 58; as more passable and more medical modifications 59–62; and medical support 59–60; as more progressive, more visually ambiguous, or incongruent 62–66; and academic support 62–63; and authenticity 66–68; and class status 68–71; and geographic location 71–72; and racism 72–80; as self-defeating 80–82

trans* female an individual who was assigned male at birth, but identifies as female. Sometimes called male-to-female or MTF transsexuals: xii, 1; and violence 156–160

trans* male an individual who was assigned female at birth, but identifies as male. Sometimes called female-to-male or FTM transsexuals: xii, 9

transgender often used as an umbrella term for a wide variety of sex and gender non-conforming behaviors from cross-dressing to combining femininity and masculinity to medically modifying the sex of the body: ix, 19–24, 128, 157, 161

transracial here refers to family members who are racially classified in a different manner than each other. Twine (2010) refers to transracial mothers, meaning White mothers of multiracial (White/Black) children: 32.

transsexual people who medically change the sex aspects of their bodies to better fit with their sense of self: ix; and travestí 3; and gender theory 15; and sex/gender conflation 18, 20; and transition 43; and hierarchies 58–61; and identification 90; and dating 98; and genital surgery 145

rans* studies 6, 18–20

travestí 3